# ASKING THE FATHER

# Asking the Father

## A Study of the
## Prayer of Petition

*Gabriel Daly* OSA

DOMINICAN PUBLICATIONS

First published (1982) by
Michael Glazier, Inc. and Dominican Publications

This edition published (2014) by
Dominican Publications
42 Parnell Square
Dublin 1

ISBN 978-1-905604-24-1

British Library Cataloguing in Publications Data.
A catalogue record for this book is available
from the British Library.

Origination by Dominican Publications
Cover design: David Cooke

Printed in Ireland by
Sprint-print, Rathcoole, Co. Dublin

# Contents

# Preface to the 2014 edition

IWROTE THIS little book over thirty years ago in response to a request to contribute to a series of books on prayer. It was clear from the start that this book would be a short reflection on God, since it had to face the question of what happens when we ask a favour of God. There is no mystery about our side of the question: we are all only too aware of our constant needs. The action of God the Creator is not so clear.

Some Christians see no problem in asking God for favours. God is there. God loves us and takes an interest in all we do. So of course God listens to our petitions, and then decides whether to grant them or not. We may find it difficult to understand why God may refuse to do what we ask; but, being infinitely wise, God sees the whole picture while we see only a small part of it. So we express our thanks if what we ask is granted and accept the will of God, if it is not.

Some people can pray in this way and are praised for their faith. However, there are others who cannot do so and who consequently and mistakenly may feel that their faith is weak. They find it impossible, with integrity, to approach God to intervene miraculously in the natural course of things and they console themselves with the thought that they can practise other kinds of prayer, like praise or adoration, that are free of these difficulties. This book is written with them in mind.

The plain fact is that prayer of petition raises in an acute form the question of God, who God is and how God the Creator acts, insofar as it is given to creatures to have some understanding of these matters. This is really a book about God that tries to tackle some of the problems of belief in God in the modern world. I fully respect those who can pray without attending to these problems, but I ask them to recognise that there are others who cannot. The Christian Church is broad enough to contain both types of faith.

# Foreword

THIS IS NOT a book on how to pray. It is an enquiry into one kind of prayer, namely, petition, and it tries to come to grips with some of the questions and difficulties which can arise for critically minded believers when they stop to ask what they are doing when they ask God for favours.

It might be thought that such questions and difficulties belong exclusively to theology and have no place in the actual practice of prayer. In point of fact, however, prayer not only tests our theological attitudes; it provides the clearest indicator to what we really believe. Prayer of petition is a remarkably effective test of our attitude to God. What, for example, would be the point of subscribing to a sound trinitarian theology, if in prayer we were approaching God, unconsciously perhaps, as a capricious tyrant?

Petitionary prayer, responsibly understood and lovingly practised, can have a unifying effect upon our life and faith. It keeps us constantly aware that a loving Father presides over and enters into every facet of life, however lowly. It does not, however, remove the questions and difficulties which face any thoughtful believer, and it should not be used as an occasion for repressing them. Reflection upon petitionary prayer confronts us eventually with the dark mystery of pain and suffering. We are called upon to affirm the presence and care of a loving Father at the heart of a tear-soaked world. Constant meditation upon this awesome theme will help to prevent our prayer from degenerating into sentimentality or dependence upon the unpredictabilities of a passing religious euphoria. Equally important is the conviction that at the heart of a suffering world there is a God who has revealed himself as infinitely more than an omnipotent creator. Christian prayer begins from a consciousness of the fatherhood of God and has its model in the prayer which Jesus gave his friends.

Because the whole character of petitionary prayer is shaped and directed by the idea we have formed for ourselves since childhood of the God to whom we pray, I have devoted the opening chapter to a consideration of this topic before turning expressly to petition. Furthermore, because theology and prayer not only feed each other but together feed, and are fed by, our concern for justice and reconciliation in the world, the final chapter reflects on prayer, politics and forgiveness.

# 1

---

# Knowing God

CONSIDERED restrictively from the standpoint of the one who prays, prayer of petition might reasonably be considered a relatively minor, and by some people, unimportant topic. As soon, however, as one begins to ponder its implications and ramifications, it quickly and disturbingly grows into a very large topic indeed. In the last analysis, enquiry into petitionary prayer is an enquiry into God – a thought which should deter all but the foolhardy. To talk about God requires two basic states of mind and heart: the spirit of adoration and a lively sense of futility. The two go closely together and complement each other. 'If God does not exist then all is possible,' says one of Dostoyevsky's characters. The converse proposition might run, If God does exist, then not to worship him is an absurdity as well as a dereliction of duty.

It requires courage to be either a real atheist or a real believer. This is why there are so many floating voters. The real atheist *affirms* the non-existence of God and sets about living bravely in the absurd flux of existence without meaning. He has to make his own meaning. If he fails, he will be hard put to it to avoid the psychiatrist's couch. If he succeeds, he will in a sense have made his own God, because God is meaning. To the believer God discloses himself as love, which is supreme meaning. The real believer *affirms* God and thus commits himself to a life of prayer and an unremitting search for the God he affirms. He would not be seeking God if he had not already found him.

Blaise Pascal, who made that last observation, has been shabbily treated by many of his fellow Christians. The predominantly Aristotelian cast of the Catholic mind from the thirteenth to the twentieth century had little time for mystics, those men and women who saw too deeply to see clearly. It therefore excluded them by promotion. We were encouraged to admire them from afar but not to introduce their thought into our theology. Blaise Pascal was that most fascinating of religious persons, a scientist who was also a mystic. As a mathematician of genius he constantly demonstrated the elegant clarity of his mind. Descartes, with the careless arrogance that philosophers can sometimes display, had said that a vacuum was repugnant to nature. Pascal, as a good scientist, said that the only way to find out was to carry out an experiment. The question for him was not whether a vacuum is *a priori* possible or impossible, but whether it *does* exist in certain circumstances.

Pascal was a scientist who proclaimed the limits as well as the autonomy of science. He distrusted the philosophers who prevailed in the Church because he considered many of them to be bad scientists and bad religious thinkers. They told scientists what could and could not be found in nature; and they told believers what could and could not be found about God. In both cases they were often proved wrong by the facts.

At the age of thirty-one, Pascal, already internationally famous as a scientist, an honoured member of French society, and a celebrated commentator on many aspects of French life, underwent an experience which he came to regard as the most important of his life. He describes it thus:

> The Year of Grace 1654.
> Monday, 23 November … From about half past ten in the evening until half past midnight.
>
> Fire
>
> 'God of Abraham, God of Isaac, God of Jacob', not of philosophers and scholars.
> Certainty, certainty, heartfelt, joy, peace.
> God of Jesus Christ.

The document in which these words are recorded is known as Pascal's *Memorial* and he carried it with him wherever he went. It was the record of his conversion, not from a life of spectacular sin, but from a life of what he himself called 'worldliness' and what later theologians would call 'inauthenticity'. The terms which Pascal chooses to describe God are an index to what he saw as the crucial element in his conversion. Putting it a little brutally we might say that he was converted from the God of the philosophers and scholars to the God of Abraham. It was not a view of conversion likely to endear him to philosophers and scholars. Why should their God have been so peremptorily rejected? Nor was it the sort of remark calculated to win him a place in the textbooks of Catholic spiritual theology. (Neo-thomists used to refer to the baleful Pascal, '*le funeste Pascal*'.)

Pascal knew perfectly well that the God postulated by reason and the God embraced in faith are not two distinct Gods. What then was he trying to say by his distinction? What Pascal was saying is that speculative reason can indeed point us to God, but its God is an object merely to be talked about. Philosophy can give us a God who exists – but to what purpose? A century later Voltaire was to put forward the credo of his fellow deists: 'Believe in God but refuse to speak of his nature.' In Pascal's view God is revealed through our commitment to him. Voltaire, who had no time for anything so vulgar and inelegant as commitment, disliked Pascal intensely. Let there be a cool and dispassionate acknowledgement that there is a God, but keep him strictly uninvolved with his creation. 'God created us in his own image,' said Voltaire, 'and we have returned the compliment.' Just look, he says, at the God which Christianity has given us – a God of war and bloodshed, a God in the service of whom Christians are prepared to butcher each other.

Of course Voltaire can be answered. We know Chesterton's remark about Christianity not having failed but rather not having been tried. It is an answer of a kind; but it does not meet the full thrust of Voltaire's objection. When I say 'I believe in God,' it says very little about me or my beliefs. I can quite reasonably be asked to say what sort of God I believe in. There have been presentations of God put forward, even by Christians, which would make one glad to be an atheist. What kind of God? will always be an important, indeed *the* important, question. Equally, should someone announce that they do not believe in God, it may be important to ask what kind of God do they not believe in.

Pascal's distinction alerts us to the importance of mystery not merely in Christian theology but in Christian spiritual life. Gabriel Marcel was thinking along the same lines as Pascal when he made his own distinction between a problem and a mystery. A problem is a phenomenon viewed from the outside; a mystery is the same phenomenon lived in and viewed from the inside.

The existence of evil and suffering in the world can be made into a powerful argument against the existence of God. If we withhold belief in God until we have found an answer to this argument, we are attempting to confront a problem. If we believe in and say 'yes' to God, then such problems as suffering become for us a mystery; but this does not make them less problematic or less scandalous. Faith in God makes it possible for the believer to accept that evil and suffering have an ultimate meaning even though he or she cannot say what that meaning is. A mystery is a problem of ultimate concern made habitable by grace and faith. The problem remains; but instead of being employed as an argument against faith, it is accepted with loving if not willing incomprehension.

Faith does not enable the believer to give a rational justification of evil and suffering to a non-believer. Purely philosophical attempts to give evil and innocent suffering a justification are usually unsatisfying, while purely pious ones are often insensitive and shallow. In no matter more than this is a wise and anguished silence the fittest response. Christian mysteries do not exist to be solved but to be lived in; and there is no way we can justify this stance by purely rational argument.

This is where the scholastic distinction between faith and 'natural' knowledge was so seriously defective. It treated faith as additional knowledge provided by God on the strength of his revealing authority. Faith, however, is not additional knowledge; it is a new perspective on the knowledge we already have through 'natural' sources.

Nearly a century ago Lucien Laberthonnière, the French priest and philosopher, wrote

> Being Christian does not mean adding supernatural thoughts and acts to natural thoughts and acts; it means imparting a supernatural character to all our thoughts and acts. It is, as it were,

a raising of our entire being to a new power.[1]

In this way of thinking there is no gap between nature and grace. Grace suffuses and transforms nature. This is what Jesus meant by the Kingdom of God and what Paul meant by the new creation. Grace cannot exist or function on its own: it has to be expressed in persons, in personal relationships, in human events, and in all the elements of material creation which provide the environment for human life and development. There is no part of creation which grace cannot illuminate.

On the night of Monday, 23 November, 1654 Pascal did not receive an additional quota of knowledge about God. He was enabled to see life, especially his own life, from a new perspective and to approach God in a different way. The landscape of his mind remained unaltered; but it was now lit by a new light. He knew better than most that the piece of paper he carried around with him was not like one of his mathematical or mechanical papers, open to scientific or philosophical inspection and verification. It was the fragmented, inarticulate, and haunting record of an experience which had changed his life. In the light of it he made his famous distinction between the *esprit géométrique* and the *esprit de finesse*. The *esprit géométrique* was his term to describe the working of the speculative, logical mind. He continued to have the highest regard for its competence in science and philosophy, but he proclaimed its impotence in matters of faith. In these matters it is the heart that counts; and the heart makes cognitive use not of the *esprit géométrique* but of the *esprit de finesse*. 'We know the truth not only through our reason but also through our heart.' The heart has its reasons which remain incomprehensible to speculative reason.

The 'heart' in Pascal's argument has often been misunderstood. It is not a flight into irrationalism. Still less is it pure sentiment. Least of all is it sentimentality or emotionalism. It is an intuitive faculty not unlike Newman's 'illative sense' which functions in a different manner from the speculative intellect. Pascal is in the Augustinian tradition of redeemed pessimism. He bequeathed to French theology, spirituality, and even philosophy a concern for the *fait intérieur*, the interiorly

---

1. Cited in G. Daly, *Transcendence and Immanence: A Study in Catholic Modernism and Integralism*, Oxford, 1980, p. 107.

given fact. In a splendid phrase Laberthonnière described Pascal as a 'positivist of interior reality'. He looked into himself and into human society and saw there a divided self which makes nonsense of the claim that God can be encompassed by the *esprit de géométrie*. He also discovered a hunger for God which no amount of speculative reasoning could assuage.

Pascal was supremely aware of the ambiguity of the verb 'to know'. He does not deny that God can be 'known' by philosophy or discursive reason; he simply observes that this use of 'know' is of no religious significance. Faith is 'God perceived by the heart, not by the reason'. Pascal's scholastic opponents often claimed that his appeal to the 'heart' had the effect of reducing faith to mere feeling. This charge is simply untrue. Pascal's *ordre du cœur* is a genuinely mental one, but it refers to the intuitive rather than to the discursive use of the mind. When Pascal says that God is apprehended by the heart and not by the reason, he means that in the things of God the mind must be used in a particular mode. It must be allied to the affections and the will so that the whole personality is involved in the process. This is of course what the New Testament means by 'faith'.

I have dwelt on Pascal because an awareness of what he was saying is particularly important in any discussion about God. To respond to God in faith is to embrace God, problems and all. Faith does not make it easier to speak about God. All the problems of 'God-talk' remain even after one has made a profound and thorough act of faith and has striven to define one's own life accordingly. That is why it is so important to distinguish faith from theology and even from doctrine. We can listen and talk to God and still share in all the difficulties which contemporary men and women experience in talking *about* God. Facing these difficulties honestly and fearlessly need be no threat to faith.

On the contrary, faith is deepened by our willing acceptance of the asceticism involved in facing the challenges of our own age. The reflective believer has to wrestle with God and sometimes to agonize over God's plan for the world we live in. He or she can do this and yet meet God just as profoundly as any believer did in previous ages which took God's existence virtually for granted and felt able to speak about him with confident clarity and without stress or strain. Once upon a time the Holy Spirit operated within this world-view where God seemed to be so easily found. There is no point in our trying to recapture the security of that world. Even if we were able to do so, we would not meet the Holy Spirit there, because the Holy Spirit, in pursuit of his own creative purposes, has moved into the restless world of our time. God spoke to Job from out of the whirlwind, and he is doing the same to us. The question of God has become an increasingly difficult one in the course of the last two centuries. The origins of the difficulty lie still further back, but the problem assumed critical proportions only nearer our own time.

One very important reason for the rise of this problem is the change of world-view which has taken place since the scientific revolution. The classical, especially the Greek, world-view has been replaced by one based on science and technology. Many of the early formulations of Christian belief depended greatly upon, and made much use of, Greek philosophical ideas. The trouble with philosophical ideas, however, is that they go in and out of fashion.

The Bible, on the other hand, does not present a philosophical view of God. It speaks of God in a very human, even anthropomorphic way. (This is one reason why the Bible rides out the ebb and flow of philosophical and cultural fashions.) Protestantism has always been less bound to philosophical positions than has Catholicism. Protestants were more alive to the changes which began to take place in the world in the centuries which followed the Reformation. They were less tied to the culture of the ancient world than was Catholicism with its heavy doctrinal investment in the culture of the past. Catholic theologians continued to emphasize the changelessness of Catholic truth, meaning by 'changeless' not merely the substance of that truth but also the mode and language employed in its formulation.

During the last 400 years the ancient world-view has been rapidly corroding, with science and technology making it increasingly difficult to go on placidly looking out on the world through classical spectacles. This change in world-view has had serious repercussions upon our view of God, of human nature, and of the relationship between the two. The God of Greek philosophy was eternal, all-powerful and, above all, unchangeable. These abstractions, however, often made him seem very remote from the world of human experience. The world (and we have to remember that this meant the planet earth) was seen as a colony founded to serve as a theatre for our redemption. Platonic exile became the Christian's vale of tears. The world was a place to be endured until death rescued one from it. When science revealed this redemptive colony as a speck of dust in an apparently infinite universe, it began to seem rather wasteful of God to have gone to so much cosmic trouble just to produce one little penal colony.

These and other changes in human consciousness have played a significant part in reshaping the Christian image of God. God himself remains unchanged, but our perception of him, in and with the models we employ in our attempts to represent him to ourselves, has to change if we are to remain faithful to what he is revealing of himself through creation. It is of great spiritual importance that we do not take the image for the reality. There is no way to the reality of God except through the image we have of him, and that image is always to some extent a distortion.

There is for Christians only one reliable human image of God, and that image is Jesus of Nazareth. When one looks at some of our devotional pictures and statues one easily appreciates our talent for distortion. The danger of images is not so much that they will be worshipped instead of the Being they represent; rather it is that they can so distort the Being they represent that they point not towards but away from him. Protestant iconoclasm has sometimes seemed to overlook the fact that mental images and philosophical constructions are no less liable to mislead than material images.

The Judaeo-Christian tradition commands us to destroy idols. What the material iconoclasts have often failed to see is that the business begins in our own hearts and minds. No one can see the living God. Therefore God is always mediated to us through thoroughly human channels and vehicles. There is no short cut to God, no route which by-passes human experience. In speaking to us and in asking us to respond to him, God, as it were, accepts that the lines of communication will often be scrambled. Some believers will interpret his voice as a command to oppress their fellow men and women, always of course in his name. Others will claim to find him where he is not to be found;

others again will fail to find him where he really is, because their ec-
clesiastical script says he ought not to be there. God freely allows his
message to enter the tangled and sin-stained world of human intellectual, social, and religious thought. No wonder some theologians deeply
concerned with the sovereignty of God have warned so strenuously of
the dangers of 'religion'. Religion can indeed become idolatrous when
it is used to speak comfortably to Jerusalem when Jerusalem ought to
be experiencing acute discomfort, and to cry 'peace' when there is no
reason for peace and not enough justice to make it credible. Religion
can therefore expect to be subjected to the chastisement of personal
and institutional insecurity.

Is not this perhaps a constructive way of understanding, and coming to terms with, the difficulties which our age is experiencing in its
attempts to think and speak about God? An age in which religion is
now more ready to accept the autonomy of the secular, the free and
mysterious character of faith, and the relinquishing of political and
social props, has to be prepared also to submit to the asceticism of an
apparent withdrawal of God from the world he is creating and redeem-
ing. The withdrawal is merely apparent. God is no less present to his
creation today than he was in previous ages. In a pan-scientific age
such as ours, however, it seems harder to find indisputable signs of
his presence and action. We shall return to this problem in chapter 3.

The twentieth century has seen a profound change in human awareness of nature and history. Physicists, once the leading practitioners
of a 'hard' empirical science, now find themselves in the realms of
mystery, where empirically-based language, the language of one-to-one
description, can no longer do justice to their own observations, insights,
and intuitions. They now freely recognise that their own subjectivity is
an integral part of the universe they are investigating and that there is
no such thing as a detached observer who can stand outside the arena
of his investigations. What a supreme irony it would be if physicists
were to become the mystics of the future, while theologians were busy
trimming their sails to a wind which had ceased to blow.

All of which brings us back once again to Pascal. The God of the
philosophers and savants will always be a problem because of the un-
stable and fashion-ridden character of the means by which he must be

approached. Such a God has to be talked *about*, and the very talking will always tend to rob him of his godhead. 'If you have understood,' said St Augustine, 'then it is not God.' This was Karl Barth's point when he said that we cannot talk about God merely by talking about humankind in a loud voice. But the existentialist theologian Rudolf Bultmann was perhaps more realistic when he described theology as sinful but necessary. We have to talk *about* God, says Bultmann, *so that* God may talk to us. Only let us do it in fear and trembling with the tax collector at the back of the church.

That is the lesson we are being taught so painfully today. God's willingness to inhabit our creeds and formularies, our sacraments and our institutions, is provisional upon our being prepared in our turn to let him be God and not to imagine that we can control him by even the most sacred of authoritative means or formulations. He is just as ready to inhabit our cultural and intellectual difficulties as he is to inhabit our creeds and sacraments. He became Abraham's God when Abraham was prepared to journey at his behest into the unknown. When Abraham's descendants found cultic security in the performance of their liturgies, and moral satisfaction in the observance of their taboos, the prophets arose to interpret their national misfortunes as a call to repentance.

> What am I to do with you, Ephraim?
> What am I to do with you, Judah?
> This love of yours is like a morning cloud,
> like the dew that quickly disappears.
> This is why I have torn them to pieces by the prophets,
> why I slaughtered them with the words from my mouth,
> since what I want is love, not sacrifice;
> knowledge of God, not holocausts. (Hosea 6:4-6)

In the years since the 1960s we have become aware that something like the prophetic situation is abroad in the Church and world of our time. Our institutional security is gone and we are being summoned by a divinely inspired disquiet into an unknown future. Once again God is recalling us to knowledge of him and to love. The felt sense of his absence and the difficulty we experience in thinking and speaking about him are our equivalents of the political and cultural setbacks of Ephraim and Judah.

This, then, is not a time for the licking of wounds, for the counting of institutionalized heads, or for flight to the past. It is a time for interpreting these difficulties and this disquiet as God's gracious summons into a humanly uncertain future. It is a time for rediscovering what, for want of an agreed term, one might call our mystical heritage. We have to exchange the mirage-like clarities and artificially induced certainties of the past hundred years for something perhaps less clear and less systematically satisfying but more authentic and responsive to our real situation. If we find it more difficult to talk about God, to preach his word, to draw up satisfying theological and catechetical programmes, we have to understand that these straitened circumstances reflect not the death of God but his plan to be reborn in a more authentic way in human hearts and minds. If the world we live in is troubled and insecure, then the trouble and insecurity must form part of our religious self-awareness. Christianity can no longer serve as a refuge from the world's agonies and sinfulness. Instead, Christians must be ready to find stillness, tranquility, meaning, and redemption in the eye of the world's storm.

Baron Friedrich von Hügel, one of the great Catholic masters of the twentieth century, gave much time, prayer, and theological attention to the question of God and to the mode of God's contact with his human creatures. He was both a biblical critic and a religious philosopher. He was also a man of deep and simple prayer. How he combined these two activities carries a great deal of interest and relevance for us today. In a letter to Wilfrid Ward, von Hügel wrote:

> Is it not this, that minds belong, roughly speaking, to two classes which may be called the mystical and the positive, and the scholastic and theoretical? The first of these would see all truth as a centre of intense light losing itself gradually in utter darkness; this centre would gradually extend, but the borders would ever remain fringes, they could never become clear-cut lines. Such a mind, when weary of border-work, would sink back upon its centre, its home of peace and light, and thence it would gain fresh conviction and courage to again face the twilight and the dark.

Force it to commit itself absolutely to any border distinction, and force it to shift its home or to restrain its roamings, and you have done your best to endanger its faith and to ruin its happiness.[2]

These sentences go far to explain how von Hügel was able to engage in all the troubled questions of his age, and yet to retain the spirit of profound and quiet prayer. Talk about God was for him 'border-work' carried out in darkness or, at best, in twilight. To talk *to* God one retired momentarily to the still centre of intense light, there to be refreshed and strengthened for the next foray into outer darkness. Notice however that von Hügel makes it perfectly plain that the reflective believer cannot remain indefinitely in the inner sanctuary. That would be a cheap grace. To rest in the God of Abraham one must wrestle with the God of the philosophers. In the world to come all will be light, and the God of faith-inspired speculation will be finally merged in the God of light and peace, because faith and hope will have been swallowed up in love.

In the meantime, however, God must be sought and met in the realm of 'dim experience'. Von Hügel believed that the quest for 'deceptive clarities' paralysed both faith and prayer. (This was a comment on the scholasticism of his time but it continues to have relevance in our own.) 'Dimness' and 'richness' were the words he used to describe the mode of contact between God and man. Counselling his niece on prayer, he wrote, 'Religion is dim – in the religious temper there should be a great simplicity, and a certain contentment in dimness. It is a great gift of God to have this temper'.[3] This is not a plea for wooliness of thought. Von Hügel made a careful distinction between religion and theology. Religion for him is 'dim' (in the sense of impressionistic) because it bears directly on mystery in act. Theology is concerned with human reflection on mystery and, as such, must be conducted in a rigorous and disciplined manner. The distinction will be worth recalling at several points in our consideration of prayer of petition.

Do we experience God? The whole Roman Catholic tradition of the past century would have answered that question with a resounding 'no'. The word 'experience' was virtually banned from the Catholic theologi-

2. Cited in G. Daly, *Transcendence and Immanence*, pp. 126-7
3. G. Greene (ed.), *Letters from Baron von Hügel to a Niece* (London, 1928), p. xvi

cal vocabulary in 1907. Such an artificial and Draconian measure was bound to produce an eventual reaction. Once the reforms of Vatican II had begun to affect theology and spirituality, that reaction began to happen. It is now commonplace for Catholics to speak of experiencing God. There is possibly some danger here of over-reaction against the dry abstractions of scholasticism.

There is a sense in which one can be rightly said to experience God; but there is also a sense in which the phrase could be seriously, even dangerously, misleading. God's Spirit can break into human experience whenever and wherever he chooses, but the mode of his entry is always profoundly human. This was one of von Hügel's central insights. He warned against what he called 'a specifically distinct, self-sufficing, purely mystical mode of apprehending reality'. For von Hügel mysticism is always incarnational: God has first descended the ladder which we must ascend. Von Hügel is therefore able to extend the term 'mysticism' to cover the religious experiences of ordinary believers, thus freeing it from its exclusive application to specially favoured contemplative saints.

We experience God, says von Hügel, in the 'sting of contingency', when we cease to be satisfied by the superficial delights or clarities of everyday life and thought. God comes to us, above all in Christ, through the contingent and the finite. Holiness is born of contact with concrete things. God is present in the realities of everyday life. He is present in the sense of incompleteness and disquiet we feel in even the noblest and best of human experiences. He comes to us as the horizon of life, always seemingly receding because always beckoning onwards. Von Hügel therefore postulates a 'theory of Spiritual Dynamics' for discerning the presence of God in human experience. 'Stop the machinery to look, and you must not expect to see it moving; there is no such thing as a science of statics for the living forces of the soul...'[4] The experience is always fleeting.

Von Hügel employs a haunting figure to describe our awareness of the infinite in daily life. It is like our awareness of 'a broad-stretching, mist-covered lake, only on occasion of the leaping of some fish upon its surface and of this momentary splash accompanying the momentary

4. Cited by J. J. Kelly, 'Von Hügel on Authority', in *The Tablet*, 6 May, 1978, p. 446.

glimpse of the shining silver'.[5] The Baron was no starry-eyed romantic. His analogy of the lake shrouded in mist makes a theological point of considerable importance and profundity. With fewer poetic overtones one might say that some things can be seen only with peripheral vision. As soon as you try to focus on them they disappear. This is a useful model for talking about God. God can be 'seen' at the edges of a pure-minded search for the truth of things and of a genuine care for the subjectivity of other people. It is only the peripheral character of our apprehension of God which makes our speech about him such a seemingly self-contradictory pursuit. Theology is a second-order, reflective activity. It seeks focus, and rightly so. Therefore what it sees is not God but only the varied human responses to God. God himself always evades the focused vision of systematic study.

Once this truth is recognised, theology can not merely analyse, but actually promote, the unthematised awareness of God which is prayer and which takes place in the darkness of faith. Discomfort, disquiet, and an occasional sense of insecurity will be familiar spirits in the life of the reflective believer, but they will have the beneficial effect of preventing our awareness of God from becoming a cheap grace. The reflective believer practises faith to some extent by mortifying his or her desire for the kind of clarity which is the proper aim of most intellectual pursuits. This mortification will help to remind us that many of the best things in life have a richness and depth which escape definition. If we learn to couple this intellectual asceticism with the heart-hunger which is only partly satisfied by the many beauties and solaces of the world we live in, we shall have learned how to make nature, art, and theology serve the ends of prayer.

Prayer of petition can have the effect of sharpening this heart-hunger. It can, if we allow it, teach us to find God in the 'sting of contingency'. When we bring our temporal needs and anxieties before God, we lay ourselves open to the most basic of all Jesus's teachings: 'Seek first God's Kingdom and all these things shall be yours as well' (Mt 6:33).

---

5. Cited in J. W. Beatie, 'Von Hügel's "Sense of the Infinite"', in *The Heythrop Journal*, 16 (1975), p. 169.

# 2

# Prayer of Petition: The Problem

WE ARE ALL familiar with the scene in a novel or film where the besieged garrison is down to its last few men and its last rounds of ammunition. The hero in charge, who has done all that can be done to keep the enemy out, remarks gruffly to his weary companions, 'There's nothing we can do now but pray'. God has been conspicuously absent from proceedings up to this moment, and he will become conspicuously absent again when the relieving army arrives. For one brief and critical moment, however, he is given a sort of dramatically appropriate relevance. In all probability some of the prayers offered at that moment would be fervent and sincere. Such situations, however, are hardly the best models for an appreciation of the deeper meaning of prayer. The prayer that they inspire might be called the prayer of last resort. 'If your knees are knocking', ran a notice outside a London church during the Second World War Blitz, 'why not kneel on them?'

It is possible to argue that prayer of this kind has its value, and that men and women have been led to God by a crisis or extremity in their lives which drew from them such a prayer. On the other hand, the effect may be merely a passing one leaving no lasting fruit behind it.

Dietrich Bonhoeffer, the Lutheran pastor and scholar martyred by the Nazis, relates how during a particularly bad air-raid a fellow prisoner who normally showed no signs of religious belief began to mutter, 'O God, O God'. Bonhoeffer did not attempt to offer him any Christian encouragement or comfort but simply assured him that the raid would be over in ten minutes. Bonhoeffer was here putting into practice his religious and theological convictions. He believed that appeals to God to intervene directly in the world's events implied a false conception of God and that God himself is patiently teaching us 'how to get along without him'. The world which has now 'come of age' has its rightful and God-given autonomy, and it is the duty of Christian faith to appreciate this. Bonhoeffer therefore gave his frightened companion 'secular' support. He did not say 'God will protect us' or even 'let us pray together', but contented himself with the down-to-earth remark that from previous experience he knew that the raid would not last much longer. To appreciate the point of this incident we need to know that Dietrich Bonhoeffer was a man of deep and frequent prayer.

By no means every priest or pastor would agree with Bonhoeffer here. Some would, doubtless, argue that extreme fear had laid the prisoner open to God in a way that nothing else could have done, and that the proper response of a pastor should have been to capitalize on the event. The point can be argued either way. Much depends on one's entire conception of who God is, how he is influenced by our petitions, how he answers our requests, and why he appears to favour some but not others.

In short, we cannot consider prayer of petition without facing what is by common consent the most difficult question in theology: How does God relate himself to the world we live in, and what is the mode or manner of his interaction with that world? An enquiry into petitionary prayer is an enquiry into God. On the face of it, petition is the simplest and most straightforward kind of prayer. Yet when we stop to analyse it, we become aware of a host of questions and problems which do not beset the unquestioning believer. To some people this is sufficient reason for not asking questions. For others, however, failure to ponder what they see as inescapable questions would be a kind of infidelity, an inauthenticity resulting from flight from the truth of things.

Christians have every right to practise an uncritical faith if they find it sustains them in their everyday lives. They have, however, no right to insist that others should think and act as they do. Parents and teachers, for example, have a serious and delicate obligation in this respect towards the children in their charge. They are not free to impose as the only orthodoxy a view of faith and prayer which may be a stumbling-block to others. Christian faith is indeed a stumbling-block to the conventional wisdom of this world, as the New Testament teaches; but we have an obligation to see that we are contending with the *right* stumbling-block, and not with a gratuitous one of our own devising.

For many people the situation is simply stated and easily practised. You ask God for something; he considers the matter and decides whether to say yes or no. If he thinks it is for your good, he lets you have it. If not, he gives you something else instead. You may not want this something else, and you may not even know you are being given it, but God knows what is best for you. In this spirit a child prayed, 'Dear God please send me a bicycle for my birthday, but if instead of a bicycle you decide to give me a grace, I will understand'. (The sad thing, incidentally, about that very human little prayer is the implied antithesis between a bicycle and a grace.) The notion of 'a grace instead' is the standard pious way of accounting for the fact that requests are not always answered in the way the petitioner hoped.

Christians who think in this manner may wonder why others cannot share their approach and why a book like this should seem merely to complicate what they see as an essentially straightforward matter. In a truly pluriform Church one would be happy to leave this view unchallenged and its practitioners undisturbed, were it not for the fact that there are other Christians who cannot accept its implications for our idea of God and of how he rules the world.

There are sincere believers who have given up the practice of petitionary prayer mainly because they have come to realize the theological difficulties attached to an uncritical and oversimple view of what is involved. They practise other forms of prayer such as adoration and praise, but they do not honestly feel that simple petition respects either the mystery of God or the dignity and God-given autonomy of human beings and their place in creation.

I want to argue that these are two extreme positions, and that there is a middle way. My sympathies lie with those who feel that they can no longer practise petitionary prayer in the uncritical fashion I have described; and it is for them that this book is primarily intended.

True prayer arises out of the person I actually am, not out of the person I would like to be. A golden principle of the spiritual life is that the Holy Spirit takes us as and where we are at any given moment and gently indicates where we might more fitly be. If, for example, I am a businessman who has been involved in a series of crooked deals and now fears detection and punishment, but who has enough faith to pray about the whole unhappy affair, I must *begin* with the reflection that God's Spirit approaches me as the crooked businessman I am, not as the Francis of Assisi I might at that moment prefer to be. And I must answer in kind, with profound gratitude that he is a God who rejoices in the repentance of his children.

This is true not simply of the larger delinquencies, but of all the petty meannesses, confusions, back-slidings, and infidelities of an average life. I must speak to God in a manner which is true to myself and my convictions. I can ask him to help me correct those convictions, if they need correction, but if I am in error or delinquency, it is within the condition of error and delinquency that I must listen and speak so that I may be healed of both. In point of fact, genuine prayer will, for the thoughtful believer, consist to a large extent precisely in learning how to make these corrections. Genuine prayer is like a turbulent love affair. It reflects life in all its richness and diversity, its moments of exaltation and its moments of depression and discouragement. Because it must reflect our real lives (not our lives as we might like them to be) it must go on growing, changing its form, at times seeming to advance, at times to regress.

To turn to prayer is to put oneself into the hands of the living God who has actually revealed himself as a Father who understands and cares. This reflection lies at the heart of petitionary prayer, and we shall later ponder it at greater length. Once we come to recognize God as a Father who cares, we cannot but ask him for all our needs. We came from his hands, we are destined to return to him; in the meantime we are wayfarers on the road towards him. The journey is often difficult and uncertain. He is always present to us, but because we cannot see him, he can seem to be distant or even absent. Nearer to us than we are to ourselves, as St. Augustine put it, God nevertheless seems to stand back from us as we make the journey. He places us, as it were, at a distance from him *so that* we may set out towards him. It is the journey that matters. We may stumble and fall; we may at times abandon the journey and perhaps turn aside in search of easier paths, but he continues to draw us back to the only path which leads to him. This is why the journey cannot be made successfully without faith.

It is faith which prompts us to petition God and to do so, often hoping against hope and trusting that our lives have meaning when we experience nothing but the bitter taste of an existence which seems weary, stale, flat, and unprofitable. We should never take for granted, as something that could not be otherwise, the fact that God has placed us in circumstances to which faith is the only life-giving response. Pierre Teilhard de Chardin has made a remark which can correct our tendency to suppose that faith is an intrinsically, rather than merely historically, necessary element in our relationship with God. Faith is necessary because transcendent truth and historical truth do not simply and obviously coincide. Teilhard saw this scandalizing aspect of faith.

> In my opinion, the obscurity of faith is simply a special instance of the problem of evil. I see only one possible way to avoid being seriously scandalized by it, and that is to recognize that if God allows us to suffer, to sin, to doubt, it is because he is *unable*, now and at a single stroke, to heal us and to show himself. And if he is unable, the sole reason is that we are still *incapable*, at this present stage of the universe, of receiving higher organization and thus more light.[1]

Even those who cannot accept or practise Teilhard's evolutionary spirituality could ponder with profit this insight into the nature of faith. Faith and hope are temporary conditions which last only until we know as we are known. Love alone survives as a condition which transcends every limitation. It would be absurd to say that God is faith or hope in the way that the author of the First Letter of John is able to say that God is love (1 John 4:8). The twilight conditions which call for faith on our part are hardly more satisfactory to God than they are to us. They belong to the very mystery of creation itself. They are a limitation on God's fatherly love, and their necessity lies beyond our

---

1. 'Comment je crois' (1934), pp. 26-7, cited in C. Mooney, *Teilhard de Chardin and the Mystery of Christ* (London, 1966) p. 45.

powers of comprehension. No loving father would keep his children in outer darkness simply and solely that they might prove their fidelity. We are placed in the condition of faith precisely because God has given us a destiny so exalted that we need to be prepared subtly and mysteriously for it in a way that respects our humanity. He reveals to us our sonship and daughterhood and, through Jesus, invites us to address him familiarly as 'Abba'. Our God is one who not merely allows, but prompts, us to call him by the familiar diminutive used by a child to its parents. We have to come to full human maturity in order to be able to arrive at the perfection of being sons and daughters of him who made the endless galaxies and the infinite spaces of the universe.

In some mysterious way the twilight of faith is necessary to our growth. This growth, or at least the part of it of which we have some experience, takes place under the conditions of time and space we call history; and into those conditions God sent his own eternally begotten Son. That is why the Lord's Prayer is the source and model of all prayer. It is consequently the reason why we are not free in faith to neglect the prayer of petition; and if we are not free to do so, we are in consequence compelled to wrestle in thoughtful faith with the problems which arise out of it.

The central theological problem raised by pondering the prayer of petition is the mode or manner of God's presence and action in the world. The problem has exercised some of the greatest thinkers through the ages, seemingly without their being able to reach any agreed conclusions. It is a problem with many facets. Individual theologians have brought to it their own personal preconceptions, dominant interests, and theological priorities in such a way as to emphasize this or that facet of the mystery, sometimes to the neglect of other facets.

Iris Murdoch has remarked that it is always instructive to ask about a philosopher what he fears most. This is true *a fortiori* of the theologian. Some have wished to safeguard God's sovereignty, seemingly at all costs, including that of radical damage to the idea of human autonomy and freedom. Others have been so concerned with human autonomy and freedom that their efforts to protect it have resulted in serious attenuation of the idea of God's omnipotence and sovereignty.

The problem has become ever more acute since the eighteenth

century, when humanity began to experience its own autonomy in, and power over, the world in which it lives. Throughout the classical and medieval period the problem was debated as an interesting, even fascinating one. Since the eighteenth century, however, while losing none of its fascination, it has in addition acquired a slightly hectic note as Christian thinkers came to realize that it seemingly threatened the very foundations of their faith. Ancient and medieval thinkers debated the matter from within the confident context of their Christian faith. Modern believers have had to deal with it as a challenge from outside as well as inside that faith, and a challenge which bade fair to put their entire system of beliefs in jeopardy. We shall consider this development at greater length in Chapter 3. Here it is enough simply to claim that for most thoughtful believers there can be no question of returning in mind and spirit to the pre-critical age when it was possible to believe in an easy, relatively problem-free, relationship between the transcendent world embraced by faith and the immanent world of human historical experience. We can seek to emulate the faith of the ancients, but an increasing number of today's Christians can no longer with spiritual impunity adopt their world-view.

Failure to distinguish between faith and world-view can have very serious consequences for Christian spirituality. Our believing and praying have to be done in the real world of actual experience, not in an artificially constructed and protected area within which it is possible simply to ignore what is going on around it. The world made known to us by Copernicus, Newton, Darwin, Rutherford, Einstein, Bohr, and a host of other scientists is objectively the same world as the world in which Jesus did his teaching and in which Christian theologians did their thinking for one and a half millennia. It is the same world physically; but our knowledge of it has changed dramatically and this change has had far-reaching implications for our theology, *i.e.*, for the way in which we must ponder, analyse, and synthesize our beliefs while being faithful to their traditional substance.

We may wish it were otherwise, but we are not free to deny or falsify the evidence. Concern for the truth of things is the indispensable basis of all authentic faith and therefore of all authentic prayer. If this concern presents us with problems and difficulties, it is extremely important that we do not regard them as 'temptations against faith' and seek to suppress them. They must not be allowed to induce guilt-feelings in us. That we experience them in honesty and truthfulness is a sign that God wants to reach us through them.

Christian history offers too many examples of believers who fled from the truth because it threatened their theological understanding of the world. We deceive ourselves if we think that flight from the truth – any truth – can lead us to God; for God is truth and to flee the truth is to flee from God. The god that we find through such a flight will be an idol, a god constructed for our own convenience in our own like-ness from our own short-sighted experience. God the creator cannot be at odds with God the revealer and God the sanctifier. The coming to birth of modern scientific and critical investigation is part of God's creation and as such should be approached not with religious fear and resentment, but with reverence, awe, and delight. Exploration of the universe is, or can become, exploration into God. In Teilhard's expressive words, 'Adoration is research; research is adoration'.

In the pre-critical age the mode or manner of God's dealings with the world excited no special problems. Theologians might write learnedly (and often tediously) about predestination and freedom, but ordinary people rarely gave more than a passing thought to such matters and were able to find God's presence and action in the innu-merable interventions which they believed him to be making directly in their daily lives. Petition to God – or, more often, to a favourite saint – caused them no problems and was in fact the dominant form in which they expressed their prayer. They asked for health, wealth, a husband, a victory in battle, a cure, success in a negotiation, deliver-ance from oppressors, and a score of other temporal as well as spiritual favours. They believed that if one's prayer was offered with the proper dispositions and intensity, God, or by his leave a saint, would hear and answer by intervening directly in the appropriate context.

The scope for finding instances of God's intervention in daily life was thus extremely wide. All good happenings could be ascribed to his favour and generosity, while bad ones were thought to be either willed by him as punishments or permitted as trials. It was *a* way of finding God, and we have no business patronizing, still less ridiculing, it. Those for whom it is no longer a real or truthful option may well be tempted to envy the men and women who were, and are, able to practise it. It had its own glory which no amount of nostalgia will bring back to those for whom it is no longer spiritually or scientifically possible. If any charge is later brought against our modern age by future historians of spirituality, it will be not that we failed to pray and act as our ancestors did, but that having appreciated the critical difficulties of their attitude, we did so little to promote a new and, for us, more appropriate attitude. They acted according to their lights; we are in danger of being paralysed into inaction and evasion by ours. This is one reason why reconsideration of petitionary prayer is so important today.

In a world which has 'come of age', which possesses its own autonomy, and the processes of which are always open in principle to scientific investigation and explanation, we can no longer appeal to occasional divine action as an explanation of why something happens. The notion of God as one cause among many lacks respect both for God and for the marvel of his creation. It is theologically and scientifically wrong to think of nature as operating according to its own laws, except where God intervenes in the process as an extrinsic cause, thus producing an effect which would not otherwise have come about. Seen in this way, prayer of petition becomes a series of requests that God will intervene 'miraculously' in the normal sequence of cause and effect.

There are two serious defects in this way of thinking. First, it reduces God to just another cause or influence in the world alongside the normal physical ones. Second, it prompts us to seek God's help only, or at least mainly, in the exceptional events of life. Our ancestors in the pre-scientific age had greater scope for detecting the presence of the miraculous. Since we can explain more of what is happening in the world, those in search of the miraculous have a much more restricted field of operation.

Furthermore, when the miraculous becomes the hallmark of God's presence, we are easily blinded to his 'ordinary' presence in life and driven to practise what I have called the prayer of last resort. It becomes virtually impossible to exclude superstition from what might otherwise have been a perfectly good prayer. In this spirit mother prays very hard that God will get Billy through his exams at school. Katy, who is more intelligent and works harder than her brother, can safely be left to her own devices. God's special intervention will not be needed in her case until she applies for a more than usually competitive job, when her natural abilities will need a divine booster.

This way of looking at human petition and divine response respects neither the holiness of God nor the dignity of humanity. It cheapens the mystery of God's involvement in the world he is creating, it blinds the petitioner to God's presence and action in the ordinary events of life, and it may promote the rejection of prayer, and even faith, by those who find it merely superstitious and childish. In addition it almost inevitably suggests that divine intervention is arbitrary and capricious. For no reason which is remotely satisfactory God is said to grant a request in one case and refuse it in another seemingly similar one. 'God knows best' is the conventionally pious way of explaining the otherwise inexplicable disparities in his actions on our behalf. Of course God knows best; but that is beside the point. The point at issue is that in supposing that God's special intervention takes place on the empirical plane of everyday life we come to think of him as an arbitrary monarch who capriciously favours some of his creatures over others or grants at one moment what he denies at the next

Our task, then, is to find an alternative way of representing to ourselves the mystery of God's providential care for all his creation, a way which will avoid the crudities I have mentioned. We shall later consider the implications for prayer of petition of the far-reaching changes in human awareness of the world we live in (Chapter 3) and of renewed reflection on the providence of God in the light of this changed awareness (Chapter 5). It is undeniable that it affects some believers more than others. Some people think critically, others do not. This is a simple statement of fact not a judgment about value. The non-critical believer may or may not be holier or more intelligent than the critical believer. This is not at issue or relevant to our question. We are concerned with response to the truth. Some forms of prayer and devotion are truthful options for some people and not for others.

There has been a great loss of intellectual 'innocence' since the seventeenth century. A universe which continues to yield up its secrets to human investigation may seem less mysterious than one which we simply did not understand. It may also seem less potentially 'sacred' when robbed of its ancient secrets. God's presence and action were perhaps more obviously discernible in the pre-scientific world where so many phenomena were inexplicable by 'natural' criteria. We today have the difficult task of discerning that presence and action in a universe which is open in principle to comprehensive scientific explanation. This is why concern with 'miracles' can be a diversion from the real task at hand, which is to discern God's hand in every facet of creation and not simply in special and abnormal interventions. God is in everything or he is in nothing. His presence and action are not open to scientific investigation, and this is why as believers we have to resist a pan-scientism which would reduce all knowledge to scientific knowledge.

Science can, in practice or in principle, explain the universe in physical and mathematical terms. But that is not a comprehensive account of the universe. It is merely an account from an important but limited standpoint. A rainbow can be explained by reference to the physics of light – but still the heart leaps up at the sight of one. Bach's B minor Mass and Beethoven's late quartets can be analysed into separate notes which in turn can be accounted for by reference to the physics of sound – but that analysis leaves their power, beauty, and evocation of the transcendent realm unexplained. Robert Browning portrays the Bavarian priest and musician, Georg Joseph (Abt) Vogler, ruminating on his power to create music.

> But here is the finger of God, a flash of the will that can,
> Existent behind all laws, that made them, and, lo, they are!
> And I know not if, save in this, such gift be allowed to man,
> That out of three sounds he frame, not a fourth sound, but a star.
> Consider it well: each tone of our scale in itself is naught;
> It is everywhere in the world – loud, soft, and all is said:
> Give it to me to use! I mix it with two in my thought,
> And, there! Ye have heard and seen: consider and bow the head!

It is that 'star' which defies scientific explanation. It differs from the stars of the sky because it does not obey any of the normal laws of nature. It is unpredictable, intoxicating and free. We use all sorts of inadequate words to describe its coming to being: genius, artistry, poetic vision, inspiration. It produces delight and wonder (in this sense it is indeed miraculous). It puts us into communication with the depths of our own being and thus it shares in the condition of prayer, since the Holy Spirit inhabits those depths, and our only appropriate response is to 'consider and bow the head'. It makes us aware of a whole realm which resists purely empirical investigation and explanation.

I am drawing attention to it in the context of prayer for three reasons. First, because it alerts us to an area of human experience which does not receive enough attention from many writers on prayer in spite of the striking similarities between artistic experience and the experience of prayer; second, because it is a corrective to the pan-scientism and empiricism of our day; and third, because it may help us towards an intuition of possible modes of contact between God and us which are real ('objective') in their manifestation yet not physical in their ultimate meaning and power.

What, then, can I be said to be doing when I pray for the healing of a friend's illness? The pre-critical view of what is taking place is clear enough. I ask God to intervene medically in my friend's condition. If my friend recovers, I thank God for his miraculous intervention. If my friend does not recover, I reflect that, for reasons known only to himself, God has refused the cure and given some unspecified grace instead. Let us see, however, if another approach is just as faithful to the Gospel as this one. I pray for my friend, asking God to take him into his loving care. I know from the Gospel that God already has him in his loving care; so I am not asking God to do what he would not otherwise have done. I approach the Father in the name of his Son who shared our human condition and who knows about human sickness from experience. I realize that my prayer should be offered in the context of the Kingdom, or Reign, of God.

This Kingdom is brought about by God's love at work in the world (the traditional term for this love is 'grace'). Grace is the divine force which brings about the second, or new, creation. It does not add anything material to (the first) creation; it transforms it from within by working upon the minds and hearts of men and women. The process is deeply mysterious and often painful. For reasons which I cannot understand, sickness is a feature in it, and at this moment, again for reasons which I do not understand, my friend's sickness is a particular instance of this general feature. I ask the Father to heal him. I have no way of knowing how the Father might answer my prayer, nor of whether the cure would be in keeping with God's overall purposes. I do not exclusively specify a cure in the medical sense; for that I would look to the doctor's skill, my friend's resilience, and a host of other factors both known and unknown. I ask for his healing, because that is the natural way for a friend to express his concern in the circumstances. This is the shortest and most direct way of saying, 'Do what is best for him in the circumstances you yourself have created.' I am not look-ing for a 'miracle' in the pre-critical sense of an unmediated, direct, intervention of God in the processes which he himself has created.

We shall return later to the question of the miraculous. Obviously much depends on how we understand and define 'miracle'. That God exercises a provident and mysterious care for his creation is not in dispute. That God who gave the universe its laws can suspend them is, again, not in dispute among most Christians. To suppose, however, that he commonly does so raises far more questions than it solves.

Theologians today are therefore usually at pains to point out that the word 'miracle' belongs, not to scientific, but to religious language. An event can be called miraculous when it moves people to wonder and praise. There are moments of grace which come often unbidden and sometimes in response to petition. They can express themselves in many different ways: a deep spiritual peace which enables us to weather the storms of life; a vision, usually momentary, fragmentary and intuitive, of the meaning of things; a joy which has no obvious explanation; and, possibly, in the case of sickness, a cure which may or may not have a clear physical explanation.

Prayer has not normally been a subject of contention between Christians of different traditions. The questions it raises quite simply transcend our denominational differences. Any worthwhile library on prayer will contain works by Protestant, Roman Catholic, Anglican, and Orthodox authors. Each book will inevitably represent the insights not simply of the author himself or herself but also of the tradition to which he or she belongs. We need all these insights, because reflection on the meaning and character of prayer exposes us to the infinite riches of the God who loves us and forgives us the sins which have produced, and continue to maintain, our divisions. In the meantime we can be grateful that such difficulties as we encounter in seeking to understand the problems and challenges posed in particular by petitionary prayer are difficulties which face us all irrespectively of our church allegiance. Such division of opinion as may arise will tend to do so within rather than between our Churches.

Prayer of petition is both necessary and puzzling. Response to the necessity may involve, for some Christians at least, the thoughtful facing of its puzzling aspects. It is not unreasonable to ask those for whom it presents no problems to recognize that for others, their brothers and sisters in Christ, the journey to God must be undertaken with an enquiring mind and a restless heart.

# 3

---

# The World in Which
# We Do Our Praying

A MOMENT'S reflection will show us that our perception and
understanding of the world around us necessarily influences our
perception and understanding of what we are doing when we pray,
especially when we pray for God's help in the undertakings of everyday life. This in turn will depend on how we perceive and understand
God's presence and action in the world. Humanity in its primitive
stage, with little or no interest in, or knowledge of, what we today call
the scientific processes in nature, was ready to ascribe what it could
not understand in these processes to unseen powers by which it felt
constantly threatened. It experienced an oppressive dependence upon
these powers for its most bask needs: food, security, and reproduction.
It felt the need to keep in with, and even to propitiate, these powers
in order to secure the necessities of life for the individual, the family,
and the tribe.

The first religions were therefore nature-religions and were expressed in rituals designed to make existence bearable. In a sense
they can scarcely be called religions at all. They were completely of a
piece with the rest of life. If, after the discovery of agriculture, people
ploughed and sowed their fields, they also felt the need to ingrati-
ate themselves with the invisible powers which could grant or deny
them their harvest. Witch-doctors, medicine-men and priests had as
prominent a part to play in agriculture as had the farmer. Primitive

people made no distinction between the seen and the unseen worlds: they both belonged to the one mysterious theatre into which they was born, lived their precarious lives, and died. The fact that many burial customs prescribed that food should be interred with the dead body is evidence of how primitive cultures viewed the continuity between the seen and unseen worlds.

Then, somewhere around the year 800 B.C., a change took place. The period from *ca* 800 to 200 B.C. saw the rise of the higher religions all over the world and of philosophy in Greece. Religion now became a *conscious* pursuit. Humanity began to ask questions about itself and its beliefs. It began to distinguish between the seen and unseen worlds. It became interested in spiritual reality and was ready to distinguish it, sharply in some cases, from material reality. The primitive pantheism of the earlier period gave way to religions, some of which – and notably Judaism – made a sharp distinction between God and his creation. The Jews were warned by their prophets to shun the nature-religions of neighbouring peoples and to worship the God of Israel as a transcendent being. Christianity (and Islam) inherited the Jewish conviction that God is one, transcendent, and distinct from his creation. It was that distinctness which made the rise of science possible many centuries later.

One quality of pantheism is that because it identifies God with the universe, it finds God equally present in every part of the universe. One of the dangers of distinguishing God too sharply from his creation is that in deciding when and where God makes contact with the universe, the religious mind may single out certain moments or happenings in which God is felt to be specially present or active. He is considered to be most specially present and active in those phenomena and events which it cannot otherwise explain. God thus becomes one agent – albeit an exalted one – among others in the world. His intervention is seen in all those forces and phenomena which lie beyond our power to understand or explain.

The rise of philosophy and the higher religions marked the first great revolution in our understanding of ourselves and our world; the rise of science and the alteration in thinking which accompanied it marks the second great intellectual revolution, and it gave us our mod-

ern world. This second revolution took place between the beginning of
the sixteenth century and the end of the seventeenth. It introduced an
entirely new way of looking at the world. It is dramatically symbolized
by one of its major discoveries, namely, the Copernican theory that
the earth is not the fixed centre of the universe but moves around the
sun as well as on its own axis.

When, at the beginning of the seventeenth century, Galileo con-
firmed the Copernican theory by observation, some of his colleagues at
the University of Padua actually refused to look through his telescope,
partly because they were not altogether convinced that it was not an
instrument of the devil, but mainly because they instinctively recognized that the telescope symbolized the end of the classical world-view.
It offended their sense of reverence for the Greek philosopher Aristotle
whose authority in philosophical questions was still formidable two
millennia after his death. We must remember that in the seventeenth
century science was considered to be a branch of philosophy, and scientific questions were still tried to be settled by an appeal to authorities
like Aristotle rather than by empirical observation.

The condemnation of Galileo in 1633 is one of the more regrettable
events in Church history. The Copernican system was judged 'philo-
sophically foolish and preposterous and, because contrary to Scripture,
theologically heretical'. There is little to be gained by dwelling on this
unhappy example of fear, arrogance, and intolerance. Instead, it might
be more instructive to try to understand some of the assumptions which
made Galileo's judges act as they did.

For centuries the Christian view of creation and providence was
controlled by two crucial influences. One was the Greek, especially
the Aristotelian, world-view. The other was the Bible understood as a
literal account of how creation actually took place, and of how God
subsequently dealt with his creation. These two influences lie at the
roots of most of the notorious conflicts between science and religion.
Our unexamined assumptions are always by definition the hardest to
change; and as long as believers refused to allow their assumptions to
be re-examined in the light of fresh discoveries and insights, conflict
between science and religious belief was inevitable. The Galileo affair
merely put a brake on scientific investigation; but it did much harm to

religion and the Christian Church by opening up a totally unnecessary rift between science and religion.

In the eighteenth century efforts were made to close the rift. In some respects these efforts did more harm than the original conflict. Sir Isaac Newton holds a very special place in the history of physics. His discovery of the law of gravity was one of the great scientific breakthroughs. Yet Newton's ideas about the relationship between science and religion were curious, to say the least. It is important to remember that he was a religious thinker as well as a scientist, but he did not always distinguish his two roles sufficiently. It is quite legitimate to view God as the supreme mathematician, but to write, as Newton did to Dr Bentley, that 'gravity may put the planets into motion, but without the divine power it could never put them into such a circulating motion, as they have about the sun'[1] is to make a distinction which is as disastrous to science as it is to theology. Newton was in effect saying that although God had given physical laws to the universe, these laws were insufficient to produce all the effects we can observe, and for this reason we need to postulate his *additional* intervention to supply for the defects in the laws. E. A. Burtt's comment on this is apt.

> Really, the notion of the divine eye as constantly roaming the universe on the search for leaks to mend, or gears to replace in the mighty machinery would have been quite laughable, did not its pitifulness become earlier evident. For to stake the present existence and activity of God on imperfections in the cosmic engine was to court rapid disaster for theology.[2]

The reason for this severe judgment on a great man is not far to seek. As science advanced, it accounted for more and more of those phenomena which Newton had explained by appealing to the direct action of God. With the best will in the world, Newton had created what is today often described as 'the God of the gaps', *i.e.*, a God who is invoked to fill the provisional and temporary gaps in scientific knowledge. As science filled more and more of these gaps, Newton's God was progressively banished from the universe and was replaced by nature.

---

1. Cited in C.A. Russell (ed.), *Science and Religious Belief* (London, 1973), p. 137.
2. Russell, op. cit., p. 142.

This deplorable theology is being perpetuated today by fundamentalist Christians who try to force us to choose between evolution on the one hand and a creator God on the other. The dichotomy is a false one and, for all its pietistic intentions, a profoundly irreligious one. Evolution is not an alternative to creation; it is, for believers at least, a theory *of creation*. It is the *means* whereby God achieves his creative intentions. Scientists, using the instruments appropriate to their craft, have the task of examining and debating its processes. If it ever were to be discounted, the grounds could be only scientific. Theology is not competent in the matter. It is for theology to ponder the findings of science in the light of faith, not to affirm or deny them.

The advance of science, together with its increasingly spectacular embodiment in technology, has in fact proved fatal to a 'god of the gaps'. Phenomena which believers were confidently attributing to the special intervention of God can now be explained along thoroughly scientific lines. Any view of divine action in the world which postulates constant miraculous action on God's part leaves itself wide open to refutation and thus leads to consequent disillusionment and perhaps loss of faith on the part of those who hold it.

MIRACLES

Is prayer of petition necessarily prayer for miraculous intervention? Much depends upon what the petitioner conceives himself or herself to be doing when asking for a temporal favour from God. If one asks God to cure the sickness of a friend and shortly afterwards his doctor prescribes a drug which works instantly, is that an answer to one's prayer?

Most believers would say yes, but perhaps for different reasons. Those who have a broad, if necessarily vague, conception of how divine providence is exercised will be quite happy to attribute to God's providence both the doctor's skill and the drug's efficacy, without seeking a 'miraculous' explanation. Those for whom divine intervention must necessarily be miraculous will be forced either to postulate a special divine inspiration of the doctor or to discount the medical procedures altogether and attribute the entire cure to the direct and exclusive action of God. There are kinds of pietism which are prepared to diagnose the presence of miracles at the drop of a hat. (One might call this attitude supernatural reductionism.) Those who are determined to have miracles will have them by hook or by crook.

Some further reflection on the subject of miracle is perhaps appropriate at this point. Miracles have, in the not too distant past, proved to be an extraordinarily sensitive topic in Catholic theology. Before the Second Vatican Council they were the foundation stone of that theology. The miracles that Jesus worked were appealed to as proofs that he was who he said he was. It was miracles which were considered to give faith its rational foundation. The First Vatican Council allocated to miracles a role of considerable importance in the process which was seen as preparing the way for faith. A denial that miracles can and do happen would have incurred speedy condemnation because of the role assigned to them in the overall structure of Catholic teaching.

In devotional life miracles have played, and in some cases continue to play, an important part for many Catholics. Saints have been expected to work them both before and after their deaths. Shrines and sacred places are often thought of as not simply graced but miraculous as well. When word spreads that a miracle has occurred somewhere, that place comes to be regarded by many as being especially holy, even though Church authority is normally cautious about the matter. The man or woman considered to be endowed with the power to work miracles is quickly, if only popularly, designated as holy. It is perhaps a manifestation of the desire to have one's God not merely close but certifiably close. Miracles give tangibility to what faith is content to leave invisible.

From the perspective of incessant miracle, prayer of petition raises no difficulties whatever. One simply asks God to intervene in the normal sequence of cause and effect thus bringing about a result which one could not, or would not, have brought about oneself by 'natural' means. The only question at issue is whether God sees that such intervention would be for one's good or not.

For a variety of reasons this simple and uncritical view of God's action in the world is no longer possible for an increasing number of faithful Christians who find it critically and scientifically unacceptable and spiritually repugnant. It is vitally important that people who think and feel this way should not imagine that they are 'losing their faith'.

On the contrary, it may well be that mental and spiritual honesty is forcing them to deepen their understanding of what they believe, though the process of doing so can be painful and, at least temporarily, disorientating for their spirituality. Those for whom the older, pre-critical, view is still an honest option should remember that there are others for whom the blunt alternatives are either a faith which is critically aware or no faith at all.

It is obvious that in all this much will depend on our understanding of miracle. The neo-scholastic definition, which prevailed in the Catholic Church before Vatican II, was unequivocal: a miracle is an event which takes place outside, and normally in contradiction of, the course of nature. This definition postulates an intervention of God not merely within the universe he had created but in contravention of the laws he has given it. In the neo-scholastic system an apologetical miracle, *i.e.*, a miracle adduced as *proof* of God's presence and action, had to be detectable *by the senses*. It was this empirical element (*i.e.*, its availability to the senses) which causes all the problems. It appeals to the direct and unmediated action of God as the explanation for some condition or event. Thus when a cure takes place which cannot be accounted for by medical science, it can be described at least potentially as miraculous. This conception of miracle can result in some bizarre and intellectually inelegant constructions, as we have seen from the example of Sir Isaac Newton.

It is because the mode of God's action in the world is so mysterious to us that miracles constitute a serious problem. Appeal to the miraculous, in the sense of direct and unmediated divine action in the world, was one way of evading the problem. It diagnosed God's special presence and action in certain specific interventions which were seen as suspending, or at least, bypassing, the physical laws of nature.

This way of looking at things has been, since the Enlightenment, the object of damaging scientific and philosophical attack. Today it is also the object of *theological* objection in that it reduces God to just another force in the universe alongside known physical forces. It demeans the sovereignty and omnipotence of God. Many believers have sensed this without being able to give reasons for their unease. It leaves too many problems unsolved while creating new and gratuitous ones. The sheer inequity, and the seemingly capricious character, of sporadic divine interventions sets up serious questions about the care of God for all his creation. Why are some favoured and others not? The conventionally pious answer to this question has normally been that God knows best what is for the good of each person. In other words, since there is no rational explanation why he should favour Mary but not John, we are forced in the end to take refuge in mystery, except that the sponsors of miraculous intervention postpone the appeal to the latest possible stage in the process, whereas those who are content to see God's providence mysteriously active in the seen as well as the unseen realm are prepared to discover God's provident hand in everything. God is no less present in the processes we understand scientifically than in those we do not understand. A beautiful sunrise, the smile of a baby, or a Mozart symphony can be miraculous for someone who experiences them in a faith-inspired way.

The concept of miracle is a religious not a scientific one. Mainline Catholic theology before Vatican II treated the miraculous as being open in principle to scientific observation. A miraculous cure was one which could not be accounted for by medical science. Yet centuries earlier St Augustine in his great book *The City of God* wrote: 'A miracle is contrary not to nature but to what is known of nature.'[3]

That wise remark has often been ignored since. The older apologetical notion of miracle was provisional upon our being unable to explain a phenomenon in a 'natural' way, as primitive cultures were unable to explain an eclipse or an earthquake, or as Newton was unable to explain the ordered motion of the planets. The fact that all these phenomena can now be scientifically explained is justification of St Augustine's insight. To the truly believing man or woman any event or phenomenon can be miraculous in that it leads to wonder at the glory and beauty of it all. A miracle thus understood is God's grace lighting up ordinary events in such a way as to provoke wonder or a sense of awe. Whether or not the event or phenomenon can be, either then or later, explained by scientific means, is unimportant. Three quarters of a century ago the French philosopher Maurice Blondel shocked the Catholic establishment with the remark that 'Miracles are truly

3. XXI, 8.

miraculous only for those who are prepared to recognize the divine action in the most ordinary events'.

It has to be admitted that widening the scope of the miraculous to take in the normal as well as the abnormal may look like an evasion of the problem to those who want to know what actually happens when an alleged miracle occurs. Defenders of the scholastic conception of miracle would certainly not have denied God's presence in ordinary events, but they would have denied that this ordinary presence had any probative value. Contemporary Catholic theologians, in common with their Protestant colleagues, tend to regard preoccupation with proof as a kind of rationalism from which the Church broke free at Vatican II.

The scholastics, however, were obsessed with proving every tenet of their faith. They wished to provide faith with not merely intellectual but also empirical credentials. A miracle was therefore defined as an empirically detectable suspension of the laws of nature. Contemporary theologians, such as Karl Rahner, refuse to define a miracle as a suspension of the laws of nature. For Rahner, the importance of a miracle lies in its power to summon a man or woman to listen to God addressing them. How the phenomenon is explained in scientific terms has nothing to do with miracle. Rahner is careful to safeguard God's *power* to suspend the laws of nature. What he denies is that such suspension is a necessary element in the concept of miracle. It can rarely if ever be proved, he says, that any miraculous event actually did proceed from the suspension of physical laws.[4]

We are thus forced back once again to a consideration of the mysterious character of God's presence and activity in the world. It is not empirically detectable except in its effects, and these can always be explained from a purely natural standpoint. It is faith not science which diagnoses the presence and action of God. If this were not so, there would be no atheists or agnostics. An event which is totally in accord with the laws of nature may be deeply miraculous, while one which cannot be satisfactorily explained by those laws may have no suggestion of miracle about it. Paradoxically, it is concern with miracle which may most serve to blind us to God's constant and never failing presence and action in the world. If our apprehension of that presence and action

4. K. Rahner, *The Foundations of Christian Faith*, pp. 257-264.

remains tied to miracle, we shall inevitably expect, implicitly at least, any answer to our petitions to fall into the category of miracle. This attitude is difficult to square with the autonomy with which God has endowed his creation and which the scientific and critical revolutions have made so clear to us. The difficulty is compounded by lack of an obvious alternative. Yet the very discoveries of science have revealed so much mystery at the heart of nature itself that we find it much easier than our pre-scientific ancestors to envisage the possibility of modes of contact between God and his creation which are just as real as miracle but which do not involve any direct, immediate divine intervention in, or suspension of, the normal processes of nature.

INFINITE BEING AND FINITE CREATION

If Newton's conception of God's intervention is no longer a possibility for us today, we may for similar reasons be forced to rethink our concept of unmediated divine action, substituting for it a more shadowy, perhaps, but no less real, one of contact at a higher and, to us, more mysterious level. Indeed a moment's reflection would suggest that the existence of such a level (or levels) is inevitable in the relationship between infinite Being and finite creation.

This difference in levels has been recognized in Christian theology for centuries, but it has been largely restricted to cognitive and metaphysical considerations. The doctrine of analogy of being, in which the recognition of God's qualitative difference from the human is prevented from leading to total agnosticism by the compensating recognition of certain similarities with the human, was carefully worked out by St Thomas Aquinas and enshrined in subsequent Church teaching, notably that of the First Vatican Council.

Although Karl Barth stigmatized the notion of analogy of being as the principal reason for his rejection of Catholicism, Protestant theology has not followed him unanimously on this point. A good case can be made for regarding the doctrine of the analogy of being as Catholic scholasticism's most distinguished contribution to philosophical theology. The world in which that philosophical thinking was first done has passed away. This does not mean that the thinking done then is now superseded. It merely means that it has now to face new and challenging questions. Most of these questions stem from our intensified awareness of the physical universe. A settled and largely unchanging world facilitated certain kinds of metaphysical thinking which dealt mainly in abstractions. It was preoccupied with essences where we today are preoccupied with existence, history, and the behaviour of matter and energy. It has never seemed as important as it does today that we should think and speak of God in personal terms – and that means thinking and speaking of him in concrete, particular terms.

Genuine prayer, in point of fact, has always thought of God in a personal and concrete way. It would be unreal (if not psychologically impossible) to address our prayers to a First Cause, an Unmoved Mover, or even to Infinite Being itself. Prayer presupposes a God who is personal; and Judaeo-Christian revelation has disclosed to us such a God. A personal God is a God who deals in concrete instances in a way which is not dissimilar from the modes of personal contact we experience in human life. Not dissimilar; but not identical either. Hence the difficulty of reconciling God's otherness (transcendence) with our historically limited existence in time and place.

Whether we like it or not, we no longer think authentically in terms of the abstractions of scholastic theology and philosophy (and it is worth remembering that relatively few Christians ever did think in this way). The advance of science has necessarily led to a much more concrete way of thinking about the material universe we live in, and this mode of thinking about the universe has been matched by an ever greater concern for the dynamics of personality in the life and growth of individual human beings.

Both these advances have placed a new emphasis on experience as the starting point for theological reflection and on induction rather than deduction as the method which corresponds best to this type of thinking. Today there is growing recognition of the role of 'models' in the deployment of theological arguments. Models have of course always been used in theological discourse, but often without sufficient recognition of their character, possibilities, and limitations.

Models are images which we use to represent to ourselves objects and processes which resist literal description. The model offers an indirect means of talking about the otherwise inexpressible. It does not give an exact picture of what is happening. Scientists construct models to represent, however inadequately, something of the mysterious processes in nature which defeat efforts to describe them literally. The relationship between a scientific model and the reality it seeks to represent is described as 'isomorphic', which means that the relationship between model and reality is not exact or one-to-one, but pictorial and analogical. There is always a logical gap between representation and reality. The model merely hints at, or gives a necessarily vague impression of, what is actually going on. If this is true of models which represent natural processes, it is *a fortiori* true of models which seek to represent God's action in the world.

A rich variety of models is available to represent most theological truths, each one illuminating a facet of one or other of these truths. For full illumination of any truth many models are needed. We borrow our models from the world we live in, with its changing cultural emphases.

Today our models for representing God and his dealings with us are generally more personalist and less abstract than they have hitherto been. This development carries its own peculiar dangers, in that personalist language can give the illusion of being more literally true than abstract language. We can never afford to forget that language about God does not work in the same way as language about the observable realities of nature. Models do not abolish mystery; they enable us to speak about mysteries – isomorphically. God remains sovereign in all he is and does, though we, by our use of personalist language, employ human, and therefore anthropomorphic, models to depict to ourselves his provident care. Our own experience of what is supremely valuable in life tells us that God cannot be less than personal. Both our reason and our faith tell us that he is also infinitely more than what we mean by personal.

Prayer of petition presupposes that isomorphic relationship. Our prayer uses models borrowed from the everyday world we know, but God's response takes place on the real, though to us necessarily mysterious, level of existence. Thus we practise faith and trust in recognising the gap between model and reality. Faith is in part a mortification of our desire for clarity. It prompts us to trust not merely in God's provident interest and care but also in the means whereby he exercises that interest and care. Enough for us to know that he does care: the rest we leave trustfully to him. As long as we recognise what is happening when we pray isomorphically, we have strong biblical warrant for being as anthropomorphic as we please. We can therefore make human observations which would, if taken literally, be open to serious scientific and critical objection.

God's omnipotent sovereignty is not arbitrary or capricious; and to claim that he allows himself to be limited by the conditions of his own creation implies no diminution of either his omnipotence or his sovereignty. If God says 'no', it may be because he cannot, rather than will not, say 'yes'. This inability is not absolute, for if it were, God would not be omnipotent. It is relative to the world which he is creating and to his ultimate purposes for it. If he were to intervene in every case of suffering, and especially where he is petitioned by, or on behalf of, the sufferer, suffering on earth would be only temporary, that is, present until he removed it.

But why then put it there in the first place? The existence of innocent suffering is a great and terrible mystery; but however else we may try to explain it, we must not attribute it to divine caprice. It is mysteriously written into the unfolding processes of animal creation. It is not an afterthought, still less a 'punishment'. If God were to lift it on every appeal from his rational creatures, he would defeat his own purposes – whatever these may be – for willing it initially. As one who is infinitely good and caring, he does not will it for its own sake but for the sake of a greater purpose which is at present incomprehensible to us. That he can and does intervene *mediately* is perfectly clear from the facts of Jesus's ministry.

Jesus went about 'doing good', and much of that good consisted in curing sickness. What happened medically we do not know; nor is the matter important. People saw, marvelled, and some of them were thereby prompted to listen to him. No one apparently thought to ask him why some and not others were healed. He did not heal in Nazareth, because he found an absence of faith there. In his sermon in the Nazareth synagogue he commented bluntly and without apology upon the particularized circumstances of his healing and drew an analogy from biblical history. 'There were many lepers in Israel in the time of the prophet Elisha; and none of them was cleansed, but only Naaman the Syrian' (Luke 4:27). The cures which Jesus effected were not performed in order to right a cosmic fault, but out of compassion, and 'so that you may believe'. Men and women called out to him for help and he gave it as part and sign of the coming Kingdom. When the time came for him to face worse suffering himself than any he had healed in others, he asked his Father to relieve him of it, but his Father did not intervene. Could any Christian, however, maintain that the Father did not heed his prayer? The answer came triumphantly three days later.

Scarcely 3,000 years separate the primitive from the atomic age. How spectacularly the picture has changed in that period. If men and women are still on earth in another three thousand years time, what questions will they then be asking? And it will all have been as a day in God's sight. He always hears and replies – though we may experience a delay in delivery at our end. On reflection we can hardly expect anything less mysterious where eternity touches time, where infinity approaches the finite, and where the Absolute cares and provides for the contingent.

# 4

## Jesus and the Prayer of Petition

IN OR ABOUT the year 412, an aristocratic and devout woman named Proba wrote to the bishop of Hippo asking for some guidance on prayer, especially on what she should pray for. St Augustine's reply was in effect a short treatise on prayer. In it he answers her principal question directly and simply: 'Pray for the happy life'; and he launches into an explanation of what constitutes the happy life.

> On this question the talents and leisure of many philosophers have been wasted ... He is truly happy who has all that he wishes to have, and wishes to have nothing which he ought not to wish.[1]

The last words of this remark are powerfully reflected in John Henry Newman's *The Dream of Gerontius*, where the soul of Gerontius on its way to judgment wishes to ask his guardian angel 'a maze of things were it but meet to ask'. The angel reassures him, saying, 'You cannot now cherish a wish which ought not to be wished'. This is an exact statement of what Augustine meant by true freedom which is realised only in final beatitude, and it is hauntingly captured by the quiet intensity of the music in which Sir Edward Elgar enfolds these words in his great oratorio.

There are faiths, such as Buddhism, which find beatitude in the stilling of all desire. Gnostics, including Christian ones in the early Church, had something like the same aim, and Augustine had once

---

1. Augustine, Letter 130, V, 11.

shared it. It was called *apatheia*, that is, a state characterized by a total absence of passion, especially desire. After his return to Africa and his ordination as a bishop, however, he utterly repudiated this goal. In fact he came more and more to the view that we human beings are defined by our desires and delights. Without them we would be less than human.

No one is of course more ready than Augustine to concede that our desires and delights can be sinful, unworthy and trivial. The remedy, however, consists not in trying to kill desire but in learning to focus it upon what is worthy of us. To live is to yearn, for 'yearning is the heart's core'[2] and prayer is its expression.[3] Prayer for Augustine is the process of learning how to delight in God and to do his will. He finds in desire for God a virtual sacrament of God's presence; for God inhabits the yearning. Since petition is yearning made concrete and explicit, petition necessarily lies at the heart of the Christian life. Augustine therefore says to Proba:

> He who knows how to give good gifts to his children urges us to 'ask and seek and knock'. Why this should be done by him who 'before we ask him [already] knows our needs' might be puzzling if we did not understand that the Lord our God wants us to ask, not so that he be made aware of our wish, for he cannot be unaware of it, but so that we may by prayer stir up that desire to receive what he is ready to give. His gifts are very great and we are small and limited in our capacity for receiving.[4]

This was a theme to which Augustine returned again and again. He told his people at Hippo that God wanted them to pray so that they might experience desire as a gift from him, for this desire would ensure that they would not underestimate God's gifts to them. 'The words which our Lord Jesus taught us in the Prayer [*i.e.*, the Our Father] are the expression of our desires'.[5] He concluded his letter to Proba: 'If we pray rightly … we say nothing but what is already contained in the Lord's Prayer'.

2. Augustine, *In Joh. Ev.* Tract 40, 10.
3. *Ennar. in Ps.* 37, 14.
4. Letter 130, X, 16-17.
5. *Serm.* LVI, 3, 4.

It would be interesting to know what were the predominant characteristics of the prayer taught by John the Baptist to his disciples. The evangelists seem either not to have known or else to have regarded the matter as unimportant. They do, however, tell us that the disciples of Jesus were aware that John had been instructing his disciples in prayer and that this awareness prompted them to ask *their* master for a similar lesson. We know that John's spiritual emphasis fell on repentance and asceticism, so presumably the form of prayer he taught reflected this emphasis. Jesus, on the other hand, emphasized conversion to, and celebration of, God's Kingdom; and the prayer he taught his disciples reflects this emphasis.

If ever we are tempted to abandon prayer of petition, we have only to recite the Lord's Prayer to realize that Christian prayer is indissolubly bound to petition. The realization may not cause our hesitations to wither or our reservations to fall away, but it will assure us that here and nowhere else is where we must wrestle with God before we go on to delight in the simplicity of the relationship he offers to share with us.

*The greater part of what Jesus taught about prayer is concerned with petition to God.* Jesus in fact sees petition as the principal prayer-inspired link between God the Father and us his children. It is a waste of time to approach the Lord's Prayer in a spiritually sophisticated manner. Its spare and uncomplicated strength simply defeats such an approach. Coupled with the other instructions that Jesus gave on prayer, the Lord's Prayer gives us a picture as fresh and uncomplicated as the children whom Jesus cradled in his arms and blessed. In fact it is in our prayer most of all that we need to become as little children. God is patient with our attempts at erudition and sophistication when we study to talk learnedly about him. But when we talk *to* him, we are as little children – infinitely precious to him because he is our Father, and infinitely puny because he is our God. He blesses those of us who do theology, because honest theology helps to keep our faith responsive to the intelligence and rationality with which he has endowed us and prevents us from falling into fanaticism; but he smilingly warns us not to take ourselves too seriously. Our enterprise is necessary but also absurd; and it is prayer which teaches us how to combine necessity with absurdity. Nothing else, least of all reason, can. If revelation means anything it means the realization that finite creatures have been given the power to become children of an infinite God. Reason is struck dumb before such an improbable truth. Reason tells us that creatures can never be children, since children are begotten not created.

That is why there has to be a second creation in which nature comes to consciousness and learns to groan for its release from bondage to decay. It does so in us men and women whose individual desires are focussed into an immense and infinite longing for union with the roots of our being which, like the tendrils of a vine, grow from and are nourished by Being itself. Reason can tell us that infinite Being is infinite power. Only revelation can tell us that infinite Being is, in fact, infinite love which transforms creatures into children. The creature may speculate, indeed must speculate, on the meaning of it all. The child prays; and the childlike adult, educated to appreciate what he or she does not and cannot know about infinite wisdom, is grateful not only for the gift of childhood but also for the opportunity to live and pray in the sort of relaxed simplicity and trust which only divinely bestowed childhood makes possible. The privilege of calling God 'Abba' is the final splendour of the universe.

In this spirit we turn for instruction to the one person who has the right to teach us with unqualified authority, because God was in him reconciling creation to himself and offering to us the word and assurance of divine humanity.

The first and greatest truth he taught is that God is our Father. We shall leave further and fuller consideration of this great truth until the next chapter. Here we shall ponder the other elements in Jesus's teaching on the practice of prayer and in the prayer he gave us as a model for all our praying.

(1) We are to pray with persistence and reiteration. Jesus emphasizes this point with two parables. The first portrays a man who urgently needs bread to feed an unexpected guest after nightfall. He goes to a friend's house and persuades him out of a comfortable bed to provide the bread (Luke 11:5-8). In the second scene (we can scarcely call it a story) a very determined litigant woman approaches a worldly and cynical judge and leaves him in no doubt that she will make his life a misery until he hears her case (Luke 18:1-5). As models for the man-

ner of our approach to God these stories seem to have a certain levity about them. They certainly lack solemnity and must have been told with a smile and listened to with companionable laughter.

But their point could hardly have been clearer. The Father who already knows our needs wants to be importuned for, not informed about, those needs. The Syro-Phoenician woman practised these tactics on Jesus himself – and got what she wanted, as much, one feels, for her wit as for her persistence. The short and amusing debate between herself and Jesus is one of the most delightful scenes in the gospel (Matthew 15:21-8). There is an element of nagging in all this, but the nagging is laced with humour.

Perhaps there ought to be more badinage in our dealings with God. If we can see the humour in even the serious situations in life, are we to suppose that God always preserves a straight face? And if so, why reserve our wit for our friends while off-loading our solemnity on God? If he keeps us coming back, maybe it is because he wants our company and knows that an appeal to our unfailing self-interest is the best way to get it.

(2) We are to live, and therefore to pray, without anxiety. The biblical word *merimna* does not mean what psychologists tend to mean by 'anxiety' today. Psychologically interpreted, anxiety is unfocused, undifferentiated, diffused. The gospel word presupposes specific worries and means fussing and fretting over them. Thus Jesus says to Martha, 'Martha, Martha, you fuss about everything.' (Luke 10:41) If our petitions are to be made with persistence and reiteration, they are also to be made with calmness and relaxation.

Part of the importance of petition lies for us precisely in *learning* through prayer how to acquire this calmness and relaxation of spirit. In prayer we can learn how to face our deepest fears by naming them in the presence of God. The prospect of death, of crippling sickness of mind or body, of loss of repute or status, of estrangement from those we love – and the hundred other secret fears that oppress different people in different ways and for different reasons – provide endless opportunities for fretting. To pray to be released from them is the most natural thing in the world, and God's answer to our prayer may consist very largely in teaching us how to conquer them or simply to live with them peacefully, because naming them to a Father who cares can draw their sting. Clearly there is a most important psychological dimension to all this, for we can indeed gain relief and help by naming our fears and anxieties to friends and counsellors. Naming them in prayer, however, adds the further and all-important dimension of ultimacy and transcendent trust and makes of them a means of communication with God, so that through them he teaches us the peace which no counsellor, however skilled, can give. Prayer of petition made with quiet confidence and without anxiety can have a therapeutic effect on our lives.

This needs to be said in view of the fact that some Christians regard such efforts as 'natural' rather than 'supernatural' and are inclined to disparage as 'reductionist' any recognition of the psychological benefits of prayer. Reductionism, however, occurs only when we reduce the supernatural dimension of our faith to merely natural phenomena without remainder. It will be no temptation to anyone who has a sound theology of the relationship between life and grace, between the first and the second creation, and between the work of God as creator and God as healer. The second creation is not an additional terrace above the first creation. It is the first creation lit by a new light which gives it new meaning and new possibilities undreamt of by our unaided and ungraced reason. Petitionary prayer has a vital role to play in bringing about the second creation. That is why the controlling petition in the Lord's Prayer is 'Thy kingdom come'.

(3) When we pray we are not to multiply words like the heathen (Matthew 6:7). There was a time not so long ago when certain types of prayer which were in vogue among Catholics did not always conform to this teaching of our Lord. Conditions concerning time, place, duration and formula were considered to contribute to the efficacy of certain specified prayers. The prayer itself might have been theologically unexceptionable (though some undoubtedly were not) but the conditions for its use made it an exercise in rank superstition masquerading as faith and piety. Certain religious objects were used in such a manner as to turn them into totems.

The very sacraments themselves could be thought of, administered, and received in a way which often failed to respect their transcendent reference and reduced them in effect to the level of magic. Because of a serious misunderstanding and misapplication of a great classical theological dictum ('The sacraments produce their effect by virtue of their intrinsic power [*ex opere operato*] and not by virtue of the personal dispositions of the minister [*ex opere operantis*]'), they were sometimes considered to produce a result by virtue of correct intention and performance alone. The result was an obsession with validity which often made their administration a source of torment to the scrupulous and amounted in practice to an exercise in magic. This tendency has now largely disappeared, but we have perhaps still to learn all the lessons of how it ever came about.

Catholic tradition has always appreciated the need for tangibility and concreteness of circumstance in public worship, both liturgical and unofficial. Its forms of worship have thus engaged not just the mind but the imagination – a fact which has contributed greatly to its popular appeal. Protestantism has traditionally appreciated the danger of this appeal and, in the old days of inter-church polemic, made free with the charge of 'superstition' and 'idolatry' to describe Catholic attitudes to prayer and worship. Protestants therefore called for a refined purity of intention and greater regard for the transcendence and sovereignty of God. They considered that Catholics were dealing in 'cheap grace', that is, in a doctrine and practice of divine availability which seemed to them to cheapen the mystery of God's relationship with us and to rob it of its moral seriousness and faith-inspired context. Polemic widened the gap between both positions, and each defined its self-understanding by excluding the valid insights of the other.

Today the ecumenical movement is prompting us to appreciate the concerns and values of both traditions. The ideal is sometimes represented in Paul Tillich's phrase, 'Catholic substance and Protestant principle'. 'Catholic substance' respects the tangible and symbolic character of God's approach to us but is liable to invest its symbols with an almost material power. 'Protestant principle' is concerned to protect God's radical independence and transcendence of the symbols we use, but is liable to an excess of iconoclasm and puritanism. Catholicism appreciates the need for fibre in our spiritual diet, while Protestantism warns that fibre alone has no nutritional value. A future united Church will need both insights.

(4) We are to pray in Jesus's name. In effect this means recalling his person and work and joining our prayers to his as, on the Father's right hand, he makes his intercession for his fellow human beings. He knows from the inside what it is to be human, the hopes and the fears, the exultation and the disappointments, in a word, the sheer vulnerability and contradictions of being human. In the days of his life on earth he knew what it was to have a vision and to be baulked in the achieving of it by the lack of imagination and sensibility, the petty-mindedness and sometimes the sheer malice of his fellow human beings. He knew what it was to feel pity and compassion for the oppressed and he also knew the frustration of seeing his hopes for their liberation dashed by the professional religiosity of God's institutionalised representatives. He saw suffering around him and experienced it within himself. He lived and prayed through the anguish of his rejection by those to whom he ministered.

Then and ever since, his fellow human beings have seen, approved, and applauded the vision he gave them, but having approved and applauded, having felt the excitement of what might be, have remained weary and half-hearted supporters of what is. In Kierkegaard's words, many Christians, instead of becoming lovers, remain 'mediocre patrons'.

We make our prayer through him who is God's final word to us and our noblest and most complete answer to that word. To nourish our hope and stimulate our determination we need to remember both sides of the divine-human mystery which were expressed in him. He embodied in his very person God's offer of peace, justice and reconciliation. But he also embodied our human response to that offer in the most perfect way possible to us. He gave us a vision which chimes with our inmost and noblest longings. For a brief moment in first century Galilee he showed how it could be lived so that we might have no further excuse for praising it as a noble ideal while proclaiming its impossibility in practice.

Therefore when we pray for happiness, as we implicitly do when we make any petition, 'we make our prayer through Jesus Christ', remembering the happiness which he celebrated not only with his disciples but with a motley collection of society's rejects to whom he had given the dignity and self-esteem that come from loving acceptance.

(5) That happiness was expressed in his vision of a kingdom where God would reign, where light would triumph over darkness, and where men and women would rejoice in the possibilities he held out to them. This is the most important single element, controlling as it does all else, in his teaching. It is also the key to an understanding of what we are doing when we engage in prayer of petition.

The teaching of Jesus centred upon the Kingdom, or Reign, of God. Prayer for its coming is the central and controlling petition in the Lord's Prayer. Most of his parables are concerned with it, and their ambiguity about its coming teases the mind. It is in wrestling with Jesus's vision of the Kingdom that we enter into the mystery of God's dealings with his creation. There is a creation *so that* there may be a Kingdom of God.

Some biblical scholars have represented the Kingdom as lying totally in the future. Some of the parables, together with the sorry record of human history, support this view which sees the life of Jesus himself as a failure, a great promise which came to nothing on a hill outside Jerusalem. On the other hand, some parables speak of the Kingdom as already present in the person and teaching of Jesus. In Jesus of Nazareth God lives and rules. The Fourth Gospel portrays God's reign as being fully embodied in Jesus. To see him is to see the Father whose glory is at once revealed and concealed in him. The men and women to whom he comes may refuse to receive him, but God's purposes are not thereby defeated. He reigns from the Cross, majestic in the degradation inflicted upon him by those he came to save. His last cry is not of desolation but of triumph in the fulfilment of his Father's mission. The battle is over, hell's army has fled, and there remains only the 'mopping-up' operations of subsequent human history.

It is a stirring vision, this turning of human defeat into divine victory. From the Fourth Gospel and the letters of Paul it has entered into Christian traditional consciousness. Many, perhaps most, biblical commentators appreciate the need to blend both views in their attempt to shape a theology of the Kingdom. We do not have to choose between a Kingdom which has still to come and one which is here already. The

New Testament, taken as a whole, summons us to the task of combining both perspectives: the Kingdom has yet to come in its fullness, but it is already present in principle and in grace. The victory of the dying and risen Christ has taken place, but the transformation of first into second creation requires a larger canvas than the span of a life – even a divinely human life. As with so much else in Christian faith and theology, we have to learn to live gracefully with the tension produced by bringing together the historical realities of life in the world with the mystical interpretation of their ultimate meaning.

All that the New Testament writers meant by the Kingdom of God has taken place in the person and life of Jesus and in the situations of forgiveness, conversion, and acceptance brought about by his preaching and good deeds; but the work has to be done anew in every age and in every life. We are saved by faith; but no one can do our believing for us. Consequently, we have been instructed to pray for the coming of the Kingdom. It must, however, strike us to wonder why we should ask God to bring about something which only he can do and which he intends to do anyway.

The answer is surely that we cannot ask for the coming of the Kingdom without at the same time being reminded of our own role in its coming. To pray for the coming of the Kingdom is to accept that mystery of God's purpose and to associate ourselves with it. Every petition in the Lord's Prayer and, *a fortiori*, every other possible petition is subordinate to prayer for the coming of the Kingdom. That is something we have to learn slowly, and often painfully, by pondering its meaning as we pray for its coming. That is why our prayer has to be constantly reiterated: because the lesson is given to us over a lifetime, and each of us has to live it through for himself or herself.

Hence, whenever we ask God for a temporal favour, and especially when we do so in the name of Jesus, we make our petition against the backdrop of eternal truth, whether we appreciate this or not. Or, as theologians like to put it, all Christian prayer is of its nature eschatological. It brings our own passing moment into the perspective of God's eternal now. Whenever we forget this truth (and the pressure of temporal needs easily makes us do so) our prayer loses its faith-inspired context and becomes trivial and anthropomorphic. In theory, a prayer that Magnolia, running at 100 to 1 in the 3:30, may win *could* be related to the Kingdom; in practice, such a prayer will probably be a crude exercise in frivolity (even if my shirt is on Magnolia) since the Kingdom – to adapt Chesterton's *mot* – is concerned with the equality of human beings and not with the inequality of horses.

It is therefore our duty to ensure that petitionary prayer does not sink to the level of magic and superstition. Even grave matters such as the healing of an illness can be made the subject of a magically conceived prayer. It happens most easily when we expect God to intervene in the series of causes and effects which constitute the normal phenomenon of nature. We must therefore make our petitions with a proper reverence for the mystery of God's dealings with his creation. We cannot, and we should not try to, force his hand, though he himself through Jesus has taught us to lay him under siege.

There can be no bargaining in all this. Loving parents do not bargain with their children or allow their children to bargain with them over the serious things of life. Yet religious history is full of examples of vows made to God to do something difficult or even heroic *if* he would grant a certain request. It is impossible to justify this urge to placate and haggle with God, however much one may sympathize with the agony which produces it. It is wrong quite simply because it falsifies our relationship with God. What kind of father would he be who had to be cajoled into saving his child from peril or distress and who gave the impression of expecting a sacrifice to be made in return for his favour? Of course God calls for sacrifices on our part, but never as a payment for his favours, only because the coming of the Kingdom requires it.

Conscious subordination of all petition to prayer for the coming of the Kingdom is the paramount means of ensuring that petition never becomes trivial or frivolous or is offered in the expectation of a magical response. We should therefore make our requests with as much awareness as possible of the mystery of God and of his dealings with us, his creatures, to whom he has given the marvellous dignity of being sons and daughters. We know that he cares for us. We know nothing about the mechanics of that care. It is not a matter of approaching a spectator God, presenting him with our requests, and then wheedling him into granting them on our terms rather than on his. God is not an arbitrary monarch who responds by whim or caprice to the requests of his subjects. He has revealed himself as a caring Father and he expects us to behave with the dignity of children, that is, with reverence but without servility. To approach him in prayer, petitionary or other, is to recognize his sovereignty, his holiness, and the mystery of his dealings with us; otherwise our prayer is mere superstition.

Every truly Christian prayer of petition is, implicitly at least, a request that the Kingdom may come. Progress in prayer consists in making this request ever more explicit and heartfelt. 'Nevertheless thy will be done' is the indispensable coda to all our supplications. The very dynamic of life itself, when viewed from the standpoint of faith, points in this direction. All our daily choices and concerns point beyond themselves, whether we recognize it or not. To pray that an illness may be cured is implicitly to pray for the health which never ends and which includes body and spirit. To ask a favour of God is implicitly to enter into the mystery of God's holiness and purposes. It is to recognize that specific temporal requests are made in the light of God's overall design, not merely for myself who ask, but for the Kingdom which the Holy Spirit is slowly and painfully bringing about in the world.

Jesus himself demonstrated this on the night before he died. Having celebrated the heavenly banquet of the Eucharist with his disciples, he turned to face the grim historical realities which lay before him. Because he was human, he cried out in anguish to be rescued from his approaching passion. He could not but want the chalice to be removed, yet his perfect obedience to the Father led him to add, 'not my will but thine be done'. The Father answered his Son's prayer, while suffering in and with his Son as he answered. He did not answer it as Jesus spontaneously wished him to do. He responded to the wider vision included in Jesus's 'not my will but thine be done'. As the Dutch Catechism finely puts it: 'Jesus begged to escape the sufferings of Good Friday, but was given the glory of Easter Sunday'.

Easter Sunday is not a consolation prize for consenting to undergo Good Friday. Easter Sunday is Good Friday revealed in its final glory. In that noblest of all possible prayers of petition Jesus has given us a model of what petitionary prayer really is. When he responded to his disciples' request for a lesson in prayer, he gave them the Our Father;

in Gethsemane he lived what he had taught. In petitionary prayer, when we ask for a temporal favour, we do so in the knowledge that only God can situate that particular favour in the context of his overall plan for the coming of the Kingdom. In that faith-derived spirit we are shown how to ask for God's benefits.

Every authentic prayer of petition is joined inseparably to the petition 'Thy Kingdom come, thy will be done on earth as in heaven.' It does not look for a miracle, because it recognizes that all life is already miraculous, that God already cares for all his creation, and that he does so with infinite compassion for that part of creation which is made in his own image and likeness. He brings about the first creation so that there may be a second creation. Pain (which includes the apparent 'refusal' of some of our most urgent requests) is inscrutably written into the whole mysterious process. We are immeasurably privileged to be allowed to share consciously and freely in it all, though this can be formidably difficult to appreciate when we contemplate the world and its mysteries through the tears of things. Instinctively we would prefer a lesser vision and a smaller price to pay for it; but a moment's reflection will show us the deficiency in faith and hope of that instinctive reaction. We cannot see things through God's eyes. We can but adore in silence and obedience.

There is a kind of divine helplessness about it all. God and suffering are indeed enemies, but in some way suffering is the price that has to be paid for the passage from the first to the second creation. Nature groans for its redemption; and that groaning is conscious in us human beings. We ask for the removal of our Good Fridays, and we are given instead the promise of Easter Day. We ask for a species of immortality and we are given the promise of eternal life. The Father suffers with us through our Good Fridays, as he did with his own Son.

# 5

## The God Who Cares

VOLTAIRE'S remark that 'God made us in his own image – and we returned the compliment' should not be simply dismissed as the sardonic reflection of a man who abhorred the very idea of revealed religion. There is a salutary truth contained in Voltaire's witticism. We have no choice but to represent God to ourselves in human terms. We can, after all, think only along the lines, and with the materials, of our own experience. Great religious thinkers have recognized the truth of this and have in consequence been careful to indicate the limitations of our ability to think about God. If you think you have understood, said St Augustine, then you can be sure it is not God you have understood.

It is obvious that our petitions and the way we present them will be powerfully affected by our images of God and especially by our conception of how he exercises his providence over the world. Our perception of the world and our place in it has changed dramatically since the scientific revolution. As we have seen, this change has had far-reaching implications for the way we think about God's providence.

Our human perception of pain and suffering and its place in the world has deepened and intensified in recent centuries. It is probably the single most influential reason why perfectly good and sincere men and women reject the very idea of a caring God. They find it intellectually more honest to live with the idea of an ultimately purposeless universe than with the idea of a God who has created a world where pain and suffering are an integral part of evolving life.

In the great chapter, 'Rebellion', of Dostoyevsky's novel, *The Brothers Karamazov*, Ivan cries out, 'If the sufferings of children go to make up the sum of sufferings which is necessary for the purchase of truth, then I say beforehand that the entire truth is not worth such a price'. 'This is rebellion', murmurs Alyosha, Ivan's brother. And of course it is; but intellectually and emotionally it is a noble rebellion, because it is instinct with compassion and a hunger for justice. It far outshines those conventionally pious acceptances of suffering which can sometimes be heard on the lips of believers who have never wrestled with the intellectual scandal of innocent suffering.

Most of us at one time or another have heard an afflicted person ask, 'Why has God allowed this to happen to me?' There is no really satisfying answer to that question. One can only console and support the person who asks it. The mystery lies not merely in this or that particularly poignant instance of innocent suffering; it lies in what Ivan Karamazov describes as all 'the human tears with which the earth is saturated from its crust to its core'. Prayer of petition has in some way to come to terms with it. We have to make our peace with God, not simply in asking his forgiveness for our sins, but, principally perhaps, in learning to trust the very structures of existence because they are fashioned by someone who cares.

It can be a long and lonely battle – this learning to trust the goodness of creation in the midst of so much evidence to the contrary. Some men and women simply reject the very idea of being schooled in the acceptance of a love which could but does not remove suffering from the structures of human (and animal) life. Others repress the problem, because facing it honestly would threaten their perceived relationship with God.

There are, however, also those who have come to recognize that their faith leaves them no choice but to face the scandal of suffering while at the same time affirming the caring providence of a loving Father. Their struggle wins for them the right to be heard when they speak quietly about the instances of religious and moral beauty occasioned by suffering accepted in a brave and trustful spirit. They understand and sympathize, even though they do not agree, with men and women whom the phenomenon of suffering has led to deny all possibility of the existence of a loving God. They see through the shallow spirituality of those believers who remark glibly that 'suffering sanctifies'. Suffering, *of itself*, does not sanctify: it may even embitter. It can, however, by opening men and women to the grace of God, become an occasion for the sanctifying power of God. It is often our lack of vulnerability which keeps God at a distance. Suffering, by definition, makes us vulnerable in the literal sense; but it is vulnerability of spirit which admits the Holy Spirit. Holiness comes of allowing grace to suffuse the vulnerability, making it not merely a physical or psychic state, but also and mainly a spiritual and moral one because it is freely accepted. Great faith and great trust are needed to pray as John Donne does,

> Batter my heart, three-personed God, for you
> As yet but knock, breathe, shine, and seek to mend;
> That I may rise and stand, o'erthrow me and bend
> Your force to break, blow, burn, and make me new.

Adequate discussion of the function of pain and suffering in God's purposes lies outside the scope of this book. No study of petitionary prayer, however, would be realistic or even minimally sensitive which did not advert to this pervasive and terrible question. Most prayer of petition presupposes a situation from which we want to be rescued or within which we want help or support. It is an appeal to the providence of a God who knows and cares. It will be shaped to a great extent by our image of God and by our idea of what he might be expected to do if he chooses to answer us in the way we wish him to do. If the image, the idea, and the expectation are falsely conceived, the prayer will be correspondingly distorted.

Of all the possible distortions which can disfigure our image of God, the most common has probably been the interpretation of suffering as chastisement laid upon sinners by an offended God. This harsh and repellent image of God results from projection on to him of some of the meaner and more vindictive of human attitudes. It has even issued in a theology of salvation which portrays the Father as a wrathful God placated by the sufferings of his own divine Son. One could hardly find a more striking or cautionary instance of the need to keep our image of God under careful surveillance than this crude and loveless interpretation of divine justice. It is a further illustration of the truth behind Voltaire's jibe.

We all know that we often 'pay for our misdeeds' by having to endure their consequences. When one calls this process of cause and effect a 'punishment', one is using metaphorical, not literal, language. Many misdeeds go unpunished, as the psalmists often point out to God rather querulously. An uneasy conscience may be witness to our failings; but there are men and women apparently devoid of any conscience whatever. More significantly perhaps, guilt-feelings can occur which have no foundation in actual events or situations. Psychologists have often pointed out that there is a form of neurosis which is experienced as the irrational desire for punishment. Thus if God the punisher is a postulate of someone's neurotic need to be punished, it follows that a recognition of the neurosis for what it is, that is, a pathological condition in need of healing, will involve a correspondingly purified image of the justice of God.

The implications of all this for petitionary prayer hardly need spelling out. Much valuable praying time can be spent imploring God not to do what he was not going to do anyway or begging him to desist from a punitive course of action on which he had not embarked in the first place. To be sure, many texts can be quoted, especially from the Old Testament, in support of the idea of an avenging God. It may help, however, to remember (1) that the Bible is a record of *developing* moral and religious ideas; (2) that it must be read historically if it is to be properly understood; (3) that for Christians the message of Christ is the interpretative key to the whole of God's dealings with humankind, and therefore that the Old Testament must be read in the light of the New; and (4) that the language of myth and metaphor must be correctly read and interpreted if its meaning is to be correctly determined. The last point needs further consideration.

Several misconceptions result generally from mistaking the nature and purpose of religious imagery and specifically from turning metaphors into literal language. Much depends on how obviously metaphorical the attribution is. Nobody is likely to literalize the image of God as shepherd. We do not respond to our description as the sheep of his flock by going around bleating. But we can, for example, take an exaggeratedly male view of God's fatherhood, forgetting that this image too is a metaphor and that with the mystics we can properly describe God as our Mother. It is the ideal relationship between parent and child, not the sex of either, which matters here. Scripture describes God with a rich mix of models and metaphors, quite simply because he cannot be described literally, even with carefully chosen abstractions like goodness, mercy, justice, and so on.

From this radical inability to provide a one-to-one description of God it follows that any image we form of God will always, and necessarily, be a composite of models borrowed from everyday relationships. Thus the Old Testament writers called God the Shepherd of Israel because the caring relationship between the (oriental) shepherd and his flock struck them as an apposite model for speaking about God's relationship with Israel. Even our literal western minds are in no danger of literalizing that particular metaphor.

There are, however, other biblical descriptions of God which are equally metaphorical but much more liable to be literalized than that of shepherd. God is variously described as 'jealous husband', 'avenger', 'military commander', and 'judge'. A jealous husband would seem to be a most undignified and unpromising model for God, but the biblical writers use it in a particular and restricted context. God is depicted as being married to Israel and Israel is depicted as the faithless wife who commits casual adultery with the false gods of the people who surround her. Removed from the context of idolatry, the metaphor has little meaning and may even be harmful. 'Lord God of battles' is still more harmful, if literalized. To realize what happens when we literalize our religious metaphors we have only to recall the numerous instances in history when armies of oppression were led out under the banner of the 'Lord of Hosts' by men who thought that God was using their swords to chastise the wicked.

Perhaps the most potentially destructive of all models for God is that of judge. Our human judges are, for good reasons of State, remote and rather austere figures. In most countries they are costumed in a manner which is designed to produce respect and even awe. A courtroom is a dramatic place with a ritualized routine of behaviour designed to impress the non-lawyer or visitor. Political constitutions accord the State's judges a vast amount of power over their fellow human beings. Courtroom scenes in films and plays rarely fail to grip us, no matter how often we see them or how poorly they are acted. They should have become clichés years ago, but that has not happened. Judgment is often dramatic, and a courtroom normally has compulsive human interest. When we describe God as our judge we are employing a very powerful image indeed, and one which is open to serious distortion if used uncritically or unscrupulously. Self-indulgent preachers with a poor theological education and a talent for ham-acting have, down the ages, resorted to the image of judgment as a means of dramatizing their sermons and scaring their congregations into a neurotic sense of guilt often designed to lead to a hectic and febrile manifestation of repentance.

Great poets like Dante and Milton, together with artists like Michelangelo, have lent their poetic imagination and artistry to the service of a badly distorted image of divine judgment. One has only to think of one of the world's artistic masterpieces, Michelangelo's *Last Judgment* in the Sistine Chapel, to realize what can happen when an artistic genius is inspired by bad theology. The picture does what hellfire preachers do: it literalizes apocalyptic imagery. The triumphant and terrible figure of Christ at its centre seems to be coming less to save than to punish and avenge. The fact that the artists consigns his own personal enemies to hell is a reminder that the theme of judgment can bring the worst out in all of us. The artistic magnificence of the picture and its fidelity to a then current image of divine judgment are beyond question. It is an artistically truthful rendering of a religiously distorted imagination.

Thomas of Celano's poem *Dies Irae* used to form part of the Roman Missal's Mass for the Dead. Medieval in conception, it gave vivid expression to fear of the Last Judgment coupled with heart-felt pleas for God's mercy. Since it fails to reflect our more biblical spirituality, it has been dropped from the reformed liturgy. It has, however, inspired great composers such as Mozart, Berlioz, Verdi and Britten by its drama and pathos. It offers possibilities to music which no other art can quite match. Awe and terror lend themselves to musical expression; but so too do tenderness and cries for mercy. Hence the effect of a great musical setting of the *Dies Irae* is often predominantly consolatory in spite of the sound and fury of the judgment passages. No one who hears Verdi's setting of *Salva me, fons pietatis* can doubt that the prayer is answered.

I have dwelt on the theme of justice and judgment because it lies at heart, first, of our conception of what is going on when we petition God for any favour and, second, of what we conceive him to be doing when he answers our prayer. If there is any trace of the despot, however sacred, in our image of the One we approach in prayer, there will be a corresponding despotism in the answer we expect. Until we allow the Holy Spirit to correct this image, prayer of petition will raise insuperable problems for some people, while for others it will prolong a shallow and trivializing spirituality.

We are not free to disregard God's justice simply because some Christians have distorted it by making it the vehicle of their neuroses and less generous impulses. It is a biblical concept expressed in a variety of colourful metaphors, some of which have been literalized to give us an angry and vengeful God. We must simply take the metaphors for what they are and seek to understand the reality that lies beneath. To distort the character of divine judgment is to distort the image of God which serves as our main cognitive link with him. That is why it is so important for us to have a thoroughly graced conception of God's justice.

There are Christians who feel that attempts to achieve a more loving conception of divine justice merely result in the gratuitous softening of a harsh reality. They find the attentive glance of a stern and punitive God helpful to their own moral efforts and they are, no doubt reluctantly, consoled by the prospect of future retribution for the wrong-doing of others. The existence of hell is important to them, less perhaps because it features in Christian tradition, than because they are spiritual capitalists who believe that moral spendthrifts should be made to pay for their profligacy. Their sympathies lie with the elder brother in the story of the Prodigal Son. In all this they forget that their own virtue, like his, may to a great extent be circumstantial rather than intrinsic and may in fact be due to the lack of opportunity or inclination to travel carelessly or to live riotously.

Good and evil, faith and unbelief, repentance and obduracy all belong to the mystery of creation. We see the appearance of things; only

God sees the heart, and therefore judgment is his alone. We should be only too glad to leave it to him in the knowledge that he alone can administer it in the light of perfect justice tempered by perfect love. Human speculation on it is inevitably flawed and distorted by intellectual waywardness, emotional immaturity, and general meanness of spirit. Of course we are always and everywhere under his judgment, because we all fall short of the ideal he puts before us. His judgment, however, is that of the doctor who diagnoses our illness and prescribes the course of treatment which leads to health. We Westerners need to recover the Eastern image of the sick-room and thus end our bondage to the imagery of the courtroom.

We live in a world where various kinds of alienation or estrangement occur regularly and at every level of existence. Some of these alienating events occur spontaneously as a necessary process in the unfolding of living existence. A baby enters the world by being expelled from the womb – one of the most traumatic instances of alienation. Subsequent journeys from one stage of life to the next are often marked by a strong sense of alienation even from those we love. (Adolescence is the classic instance.) Life comes to a close in the alienation of death. There seems to be a pattern in all this: We have to become 'other', separated from the familiar, in order to progress to further and higher stages throughout our lives and beyond the grave.

This is how life itself is designed, and God's Word has taught us to interpret the process as a journey in response to his call. We are pilgrims, and our wayfaring is marked by joy and sorrow, pleasure and pain, delight and anxiety. The journey results in bruises and abrasions, physical, psychological, moral, and spiritual. Much of the time we long for rest and peace. We want out of our pilgrim's tent and into a house with protective walls, a roof over our heads, and a warm bed instead of a sleeping-bag on a groundsheet. God, however, gently calls us back to the road. Lasting repose is not for now. There is a journey to be made before we reach the only resting-place which can finally satisfy us. Only God knows the final meaning of this; and we must take it on his word. He gives us a promise and the constantly reiterated assurance of his love. He could indeed give us a lesser peace, but he does not do so, because in his love he wants us to have the greater peace. And so he calls us on through the valley of the shadow of death, giving us enough brief foretastes of the glory which is to come to persuade us that the journey is worthwhile, sending us him whom St. Augustine calls 'Christ our physician' to heal the cuts and bruises acquired on the journey, but asking for the sacrifice of our obedience, faith and trust. *This is God's justice.*

The world we live in is not necessarily, as Leibniz thought, the best of all possible worlds. It is the one God has chosen; and that is all we need to know. He knows that it will often delight and gladden us and often puzzle, shock, and disgust us. He knows that we shall often seek for meaning to it all and fail to find it. Because we are his children, and because we are human, he expects us to cry out to him in supplication. How could we do otherwise? And how could he fail to hear and answer? He asks us, however, to trust him to answer as he knows best. He sees the whole picture; we see but part of a brush stroke. It is not fanciful to think of him as longing to explain but knowing that here and now we lack the capacity or the means to understand. In his justice he is creating a realm where truth and love will eventually triumph. Jesus described this realm as God's Kingdom. St Paul describes it as the second, or new, creation. The passage from first to second creation is a transforming process – and a painful one. The reasons for the pain remain unintelligible and even repugnant to us.

In the earliest stages of creation when rocks are wrenched from rocks and suns are born of cosmic energies, God needs only the laws of matter and energy, and even here he allows random variations to operate in a manner which gives matter itself a kind of freedom, as it were, in anticipation of the greater freedom which will come with humanity and with the consequent passage from the first to the second creation. Millions of years ago there came a point when life evolved and, as it organized itself into ever more complex forms, there came the possibility of pleasure and pain. Finally, came the birth of mind, the drive towards giving and receiving affection, and the possibility of love.

At this tremendous point, as Christians believe, God enters the process himself in a new and special manner, offering to heal the wounds inflicted by a nature which is now, in humanity, alienated from its material origins and groaning for its salvation. In Christ, God offers healing to a world torn and exhausted by the act of giving birth. In Christ he offers reconciliation to the highest beings in that world who are alienated and frightened by the prospects opening out in front of them.

God now has conscious partners, intelligent and free – but partners capable of saying no. One single and physically insignificant human being has a freedom and a power not granted to galaxies. This awesome freedom is no merely random material factor resulting in physical, chemical, or biological mutations. These can affect only the first creation. The human, in which alone (at least on our planet) the second creation can come to birth, has the power to obstruct, but not defeat, the *ultimate* aims of God. Like a stubborn child we can refuse to cooperate. We can rest in our estrangement and wilfully increase the forces of alienation in the world. We have only to look around our earth to see all the varied kinds of alienation, political, social, and economic, which are the product of greed, lust for power, and general lovelessness. The normal theological word for these humanly inflicted forms of alienation is sin. Therefore, high among the petitions we bring to the Father must be the prayer for forgiveness with the corollary that we intend to mediate God's forgiveness to each other in gratitude for having been forgiven ourselves.

We enter the world alienated from God, but we are offered all the possibilities of reconciliation. We begin life wounded but discover that, as T. S. Eliot expresses it,

The whole earth is our hospital
Endowed by the ruined millionaire,
Wherein, if we do well, we shall
Die of the absolute paternal care
That will not leave us, but prevents us everywhere.

We are patients in the wards of life, suffering but at the same time assured of God's paternal care for us and certain of our eventual recovery. Every patient wants out of hospital at the earliest possible opportunity. Many importune the doctor and try to extract clues from the nurses on when they are likely to be allowed to go home. 'Going home' is a good image of what our prayers of petition are ultimately directed towards.

There is a poem by Cecil Day Lewis reflecting his feelings on the day his small son left for boarding school. As the poet watches 'that hesitant figure, eddying away like a winged seed loosened from its parent stem', he reflects on 'nature's give and take', 'the small, the scorching ordeals that fire one's irresolute clay'. He sees in this parting a parable of life attempting to say

> … what God alone could perfectly show –
> How selfhood begins with a walking away,
> And love is proved in the letting go.

Most parents have been through it in one way or another: the anguished appeal 'Please may I come home?', or 'Why do I have to go to the hospital?' It is a good model for our attempt to understand God's providence. There is no Easter Day without a Good Friday; and the Father would be granting an infinitely lesser gift if he responded by removing the Good Friday. But the greater gift is paid for in pain; and the meaning of this can be seen only on the other side, when the journey is complete.

This can be glimpsed if we place two gospel texts alongside each other. 'Father, let this chalice pass away' is a passion text instinct with pain and dread. 'Was it not necessary that the Christ should suffer these things and enter into his glory?' is a resurrection text radiant with joy and the vision of meaning. The meaning emerges only when the painful journey has been completed. Jesus himself used the image of the woman in labour: the pain achieves meaning when she holds the new-born infant in her arms. Life is full of small epiphanies like that. We approach the dentist with mild dread; we leave with light step and perhaps a certain shame over our earlier fear. We are painfully nervous before some difficult assignment; when it has passed off successfully, we are elated.

Day Lewis's reflection on the small boy facing his first break with home life is a sort of parable of creation. Nature evolves into ever higher forms of life until a creature emerges who is intelligent and free. 'Selfhood begins with a walking away'. There is a universe to be explored, and we have the desire and the growing capacity to explore it. The God who made us knows that many voyages and expeditions

will come to grief and that there will be many false turnings and los-
ings of the way. Yet the exploration must take place; and God proves
his love in the letting go. There will be many anguished letters home
imploring to be taken away from school and restored to the safety of
the nursery. But there is no return to the nursery without damage and
regression. Creation, with all its hazards and discomforts, must go on.
It has about it an inexorability against which we must live out our lives:
*And this is the justice of God.*[1]

The letters home are our prayers of petition. They envisage school
life as the immediately real world: teachers, lessons, exams, games,
friendships haltingly made and painfully broken, food, and, of course,
the approaching holidays. The parents who receive these letters live in
a more objectively real world and can read them in perspective. That
all-important match, the free-day, the imminent exams, the chronic
shortage of pocket-money, coupled with the protestation that every
other boy or girl in school gets far more than I do – all these constitute present reality for the child at school. It is a very limited reality,
because the perspectives under which it is seen are of their nature
narrow, cloistered, and temporary.

Prayer of petition, for all its fervour and sense of urgency, can be
very short-sighted and self-centred. Even the Psalms, those striking
outpourings of the religious spirit which are the core of Christian as
well as Jewish liturgical prayer, are not free of sentiments which can
hardly be squared with those of the Sermon on the Mount. The psalm-
ist often asks for mercy for himself while at the same time calling for
retribution on his opponents. Must we then not hope that God will
hear our petitions not only with compassion but sometimes with a
sense of humour? Otherwise how could he listen equally to the prayer
of someone who is asking him to punish the wicked man who lives
down the street, while that same allegedly wicked man is asking to be
rescued from the unjust charges of his accusers? If the farmers want
rain and the holiday-makers want sun, God's response may simply be to
bless both with a smile while leaving the weather to the meteorological
forces which are part of his divine creation.

1. I am indebted to Paul Tillich's *Systematic Theology*, Vol. 2 (Nisbet edit. Welyn Gar-
den City, pp. 200-203) for this fascinating insight.

God's steadfast love is at the heart of all that he has disclosed to us about himself. Our idea of it, our capacity for representing it to ourselves, however, is fragmented and derivative. We have some idea of what it means to say that God loves us, because we have experienced a variety of human examples of loving and caring both actively and passively. By the use of our minds and imaginations we attribute to God through mental transposition what is best in our human experience. Imperfect as this process is, we can do no other. The only alternative to such transposition is a total silence that would witness to virtual agnosticism about God. Some theologians, and most of the mystics, have warned us about what we do *not* know about God. It is a warning we forget at our peril. To believe that God has sent his Word into history, however, is to forswear the elegant silence enjoined by some philosophers on the grounds that what we cannot talk about adequately we should not talk about at all.

However inadequate and distorted our idea of God may be, under proper nurture and control it is enough to fuel faith and nourish prayer. We have quite simply to accept the inadequacy and the distortion in the conviction that God can and does reach us through the very imperfect image that we have of him. He does not, however, thereby dispense us from explicit awareness of the limitations of our knowledge – that 'educated nescience' of which Augustine wrote to Proba. Lack of such awareness leads inevitably to idolatry by which we confuse the image with the reality.

Our image of God should always be open in principle to modification by correction and even reconstruction. The most obvious instance of this need for modification is the passage from childhood to adulthood. The child's idea of God cannot sustain an adult, who, if he or she retains his or her childhood religious images, risks loss of faith as his or her mind develops towards greater sophistication in matters of worldly wisdom. Every mental and affective modification we undergo in life has implications for our awareness of God, because God discloses himself to us through our everyday experiences, and perhaps especially through the peak experiences of intense joy or sorrow. Our relationship with him is shaped largely by our relationship with each other. For this reason prayer always has a social and political dimension. We shall consider this dimension in the next chapter.

We approach God with our requests and intercessions because it is natural and good to petition and intercede with those who care for us, and because he has disclosed his wish that we should do so. As soon as we begin to ask what exactly happens when God hears and answers our requests, we enter territory that is staked out by signs which warn us about what we do not and cannot know about God. We know that he cares and provides for his creation. We know little or nothing of the mode of that caring and providence. The frontier, or interface, between divine action and historical, this worldly, existence is not open to our inspection or understanding. Our ancestors were able to think of God's action as a straightforward intervention in the normal and observable sequence of cause and effect. For reasons which we have already considered, this way of thinking has become problematical for us today. The advance of science is constantly demonstrating the mystery of nature's processes. If created processes are mysterious, can we expect any greater clarity in our understanding of the Creator's actions?

What we do know is that he rules creation in a manner which respects both its laws and the random factors which operate within those laws. We human beings have emerged from created nature and contribute our intelligence and freedom to the dynamic unfolding of that nature. We are, as Goethe put it, nature's first conversation with God. On God's part that conversation is a sustained and loving call to us to come to him, trusting where we cannot comprehend. On our part the dialogue must necessarily express itself in the imploring of favours, in the expression of our fears and anxieties, and above all in the realisation that God's caring cannot always be expressed in ways which make immediate sense to us. We must seek to reflect God's infinite patience by our own finite and hard-achieved patience. We have, in short, to let God have *his* freedom, not seeking to bind him within the confines of our limited experience or to bend him to our wills. It can take a lifetime to learn how to pray with insistence, reiteration, and even passion, and yet to reverence God's infinite wisdom and to trust his 'absolute paternal care'. To pray is to go to school.

# 6

## Prayer, Politics and Forgiveness

MID-WAY THROUGH the Lord's Prayer there is a dramatic change of direction. The first clauses are concerned with God, his name, his Kingdom, and his will. Then quite abruptly we are brought down to earth with the petition 'Give us this day our daily bread'. From the earliest ages of the Church there have been those who felt that there was something anticlimactic about understanding 'bread' in its obvious material sense. Consequently they have sought to refer this petition either to the Eucharist or to the banquet which will celebrate the end of time.

There have always been Christians anxious to 'supernaturalize' everything in the name of faith. They practise a kind of supernatural imperialism, annexing the temporal to the spiritual whenever possible. They read the Bible allegorically and are thus able to convert 'temporal' things and events into 'spiritual' ones by the simple expedient of interpreting them as allegories for spiritual truths. While it is true that some of this allegorization may contain spiritual truths of importance in their own right, much of it tends to strike us today as far-fetched, in that it flies in the face of the text's obvious meaning and, in some cases, offends against the autonomy and dignity of material creation.

The prayer for daily bread should be interpreted in its obvious literal sense, if only because it reflects the potential holiness of all creation, accepts the legitimate reality of temporal needs, and warns us against the false piety of supposing that only the immaterial can be holy. Our material needs are real, important in their own right, and not to be piously sublimated.

The Greek word '*epiousios*', normally rendered as 'daily' is admittedly strange. It might be rendered as 'daily ration', or 'enough for the day'. The phrase 'daily bread', then, can be properly taken as referring to all our material needs, including food, housing, and (today) employment, with no infidelity to the text. In the Sermon on the Mount, within which Matthew sites the Lord's Prayer, we are told not to fret about these needs, since our heavenly Father already knows about them. The Lord's Prayer simply recognizes this. It places these needs in God's hands and refuses to worry any further.

Having registered the biblical meaning, we have then to turn to some of the formidable questions which face us today in trying to make them relevant to our situation. 'Give us this day our daily bread' is, or ought to be, a disturbing petition precisely because it is plural rather than singular: Give *us*, not simply me, *our*, not merely my, daily bread. This prayer cannot, or should not, be offered in pious isolation from the terrible facts of life on this planet where the majority of the population are hungry, malnourished, and living in conditions which are an outrage upon the humanity they share with us and an insult to the divine image which is stamped upon the being of every man, woman, and child among them. Politically conservative members of the well-fed, well-housed, consumer-orientated society of the northern hemisphere sometimes refer to people who express dissatisfaction with these terrible facts as 'bleeding hearts'. That coarse and contemptuous phrase disqualifies its users from any claim to being Christian, except in name, and, if they are churchgoers, they are simply adding hypocrisy to malice by using it.

The prophets of Israel centuries ago castigated the 'cultic security' of those who perpetrated injustice against the weak and defenceless and then went to worship in the Temple. Their iniquity, as the prophets saw it, lay not merely in their injustices but in their worship. Their lack of concern for justice turned their worship into rank superstition and made it a sham, since in detaching worship from morality they were implying that God could be honoured by the mere performance of a ritual divorced from life. The prophets set out to proclaim the indissoluble connection between worship and morality.

> Woe to those who turn justice into wormwood,
> throwing integrity to the ground;
> who hate the man dispensing justice at the city gate
> and detest those who speak with honesty.
> Seek good and not evil
> so that you may live,
> and that Yahweh, God of Sabaoth, may really be with you as you
>    claim he is.
> Hate evil, love good,
> maintain justice at the city gate...
> Above all, do not imagine that your worship will supply for your
>    injustices, for
> I hate and despise your feasts,
> I take no pleasure in your solemn festivals.
> When you offer me holocausts ...
> I reject your oblations,
> and refuse to look at your sacrifices of fattened cattle.
> Let me have no more of the din of your chanting,
> no more of your strumming on harps.
> But let justice flow like water,
> and integrity like an unfailing stream. (Amos 5:7,10,14,15,21-24)

These are powerful words indeed. They condemn out of hand any-one who fails to see that worship implies a deep concern for justice. Admittedly the prophets were referring to those who actively inflicted injustice on others. Can the condemnation be properly extended to cover those who, while not actively perpetrating injustice on others, nevertheless are careless of the fact that injustice *is being* perpetrated on others, often in a way which is too diffuse to allow for accurate determination of guilt?

The prophets broke new ground in establishing a firm connection between morality (especially justice) and the worship of God. They were referring primarily to individual injustice, but the social over-tones were already there, and what they said of individual injustice can logically be applied to social and systematic injustice in an age when new modes of travel and media of communication have shrunk the world to a global village. The gate of the town, which in biblical times marked the place where crooked deals were done and the defenceless were defrauded, has become the symbol of our present-day socio-economic systems which are responsible for so much systematic rather than purely personal injustices.

A small leap of imagination gives the old prophetic message a new relevance. We today have no difficulty in seeing that mine owners in the nineteenth century who kept women and children down the pits for 18 hours a day and yet could assemble in church every Sunday were offending spectacularly against the prophetic teaching of their faith. Will people a hundred years hence condemn us for praying comfortably while half our world starved?

Christianity added a new and powerful dimension to the prophetic message. The twenty-fifth chapter of St Matthew's Gospel shows us Jesus identifying himself with every man, woman and child in need. 'As long as you did it to one of these, you did it to me'. Jesus does not say, 'I will take it *as if* you did it to me'; he says, quite simply, 'you *did* it to me'. Christ, said Pascal, will be in torment until the end of time. He is in torment whenever any human being is in torment, especially in the sort of torment which is inflicted by 'man's inhumanity to man'.

St John Chrysostom, in a powerful passage, puts the matter succinctly and searingly:

> You eat to excess; Christ eats not even what he needs. You eat a variety of cakes; he eats not even a piece of dried bread. You drink fine Thracian wine; but on him you have not bestowed so much as a cup of cold water. You lie on a soft and embroidered bed; but he is perishing in the cold.[1]

The first thing that strikes us when we consider the petition 'Give *us* this day our daily bread' is that God does not appear to be answering our prayer in, for example, the shanty towns of the world. Then we may go on to reflect once again on a theme which has recurred often in this book, namely, the indirect, mediate, character of God's dealings

---

1. *On Matthew*, Homily 48.4, cited in J. C. Haughey (ed.), *The Faith that Does Justice* (New York/Ramsey/Toronto, 1977, p. 130).

with us. *How* do we expect God to feed, clothe, and house the destitute throughout the world? The raw materials are there. The political will is not. The great powers are engaged in an obscene rush to outstrip each other in possession of weapons of unthinkably destructive force. The costs are so enormous that ordinary people cannot take them in with mind or imagination. Meanwhile, the poor go hungry and homeless. That, for Christians, means that Christ goes hungry and homeless, while fundamentalist brands of Christianity flourish in comfortable security and with high-level political and economic support. And yet we pray 'Give us this day our daily bread'.

'If one of the brothers or one of the sisters is in need of clothes and has not enough food to live on, and one of you says to them, "I wish you well; keep yourself warm and eat plenty", without giving them these bare necessities of life, then what good is that?' (James 2:15-16). How James's blunt observation is to be applied at social and political levels powerful and influential enough to make any significant difference is a question of daunting complexity. Christians are as divided on the matter as any other group of citizens in our western democracies. Any attempt to discuss the matter in detail goes far beyond the scope of this book or the abilities of its author. I am doing no more here than claiming that we cannot simply ask God to feed and house the world's population without constantly asking ourselves what God might be expecting of us by way of action.

Since only large-scale political action can meet the problem adequately, *some* kind of political interest and action is expected of Christians. Donations to relief agencies are important but not enough. What we do with our vote has to come into it. 'Give *us* this day our daily bread' has to extend beyond the anxieties of bourgeois existence. We cannot remain content to put into power politicians who undertake to improve our own local or national standard of living. Inflation is a morally damaging condition because it turns our attention inward upon our own private needs. Inflation brings out all our selfish instincts and clothes them in a species of virtue; for is it not virtuous to be concerned about the wellbeing of one's own family and one's own country? The reality or even the prospect of unemployment on our own doorstep easily blinds us to the plight of those who have never been employed partly, at least, because their malnutrition would make it impossible for them to look for or find work.

The Gospel gives us no direct and concrete guidance on how to meet the challenge of poverty on a global scale. Global awareness was not a real possibility in biblical times. The neighbour in need who is envisaged in the Gospel lives next door, or in the same village, or is met on the road from Jerusalem to Jericho. The injustices envisaged by the prophets of Israel took place at the city gate where trading was done.

We have to extend the moral imperatives of Jesus and the prophets so that they cover situations that many of us have never experienced at first hand, apart from what we may have seen on our television screens. We know that we cannot respond as we would to need on our own doorstep. Most of us are deeply moved when we see some scene of misery and degradation which is taking place thousands of miles away from us. We experience a sense of helplessness which turns to frustration at our sheer physical inability to help. For a while we fret and perhaps pray for the victims who have invaded the comfortable unreality of our screens. Then we forget; not because we do not care, but because we cannot endure the frustration.

But it is vitally important that we do not allow ourselves or others to forget. Parents and teachers who ensure that their children are made constantly aware of the world's areas of poverty and injustice may well be sowing the seeds of future action. Preachers who return constantly to this theme in their sermons may irritate those members of their congregations who defend their comfortable pieties with the cry: 'Keep politics out of religion'; but they may also touch the consciences of those who are able to exercise influence nearer the centres of power than the preacher himself could ever hope to be. We can campaign on behalf of politicians who show an awareness of global poverty and are courageous enough to put that awareness to the test of the ballot-box. If we can help to bring about a climate of global concern and demonstrate that we are prepared to use our vote to back our concern, there will be no shortage of politicians ready to include such concern in their political programmes. We cannot reasonably expect politicians to court rejection at the polls, when they know that their constituents are totally preoccupied with domestic anxieties.

And we can pray. As long as we are trying to do something, our prayer is saved from presumption, superstition, or passing of the buck to God. Creation has reached a point where God wishes to work through the creatures he is calling to live up to the dignity of their vocation as divinely adopted sons and daughters. In order to respond to that call, we have to become ever more conscious of its implications for our relations with every member of the human family. Prayer, especially prayer of intercession, has a vital role to play in that process. God wishes us to pray so that our prayer may stimulate our desire. St. Augustine, who made that remark, was referring to our desire for God, but his point can be applied with equal validity to our desire for social justice.

The philosopher Immanuel Kant claimed that the purpose of prayer is 'to induce in us a moral disposition'. Kant meant that prayer was *nothing but* an attempt to stir up our consciences, and, understood thus, his view is rightly objected to by most Christians as unacceptable reductionism.

The fault, however, lies in the reductionism, not in the observation itself. Remove the 'nothing but', and Kant's remark is true and important. He was perfectly correct in noting that what the Liberation theologians call 'conscientization' is indeed one of the functions of prayer, especially prayer of intercession. It is by praying for John or Mary that I may be prompted to *do* something for John or Mary. Prayer is a process of learning how to listen and respond to God. God in Christ has told us that listening to him means listening to our fellow men and women. I have no business asking God to give me what I can, but do not choose to, give my fellows. If I am in personal distress, so too are millions of others. My faith instructs me that if I seek solace in God, I must take with me into God's presence not merely my own distress but that of others as well. Prayer of petition is always in danger of a selfish narrowness. This narrowness can be corrected by the regular practice of intercessory prayer.

For Christians the theological basis of intercessory prayer is the fact that Jesus has been raised to the Father's right hand where he intercedes for us, his human brothers and sisters (Hebrews 7:25). He is mediator between God and humankind. On earth he was God's Word to us expressed as one of us. He was also our perfect answer to that Word. On earth he emptied himself of the glory that was his due and practised obedience unto death; in heaven he is raised above every creature where he speaks on our behalf (Phillipians 2:6-11). Christian intercession seeks to graft itself on to Christ's own prayer of intercession. It tries to be deliberately redemptive in character. It undertakes to think of others in their own right and in the light of God's Kingdom. Thus all that we have been considering about petitionary prayer applies to intercessory prayer, with the important difference, however, that intercessory prayer has the moral and spiritual advantage of being concerned with others and is therefore less liable to selfishness and narrowness of interest.

In intercession we bring before the Father our experience of living in a broken world where natural catastrophes occur and are aggravated by human malice, stupidity, and concern for private gain. Response to a great natural catastrophe, say, an earthquake, exposes what Pascal called the glory and the scandal of human behaviour. People are deeply touched; some volunteer for service in the afflicted area; others give donations to relief organizations. People are ready to make sacrifices for their suffering brothers and sisters; and this is human glory at its best.

So often, however, the next news seems to diminish the hope and edification we have been experiencing from the attempts at relief, as we hear of bureaucratic corruption and inefficiency often at the very site of the tragedy. Not merely is one person's generosity offset by another's cupidity, but human magnanimity and generosity are flawed at their very source, and the flower of generous caring seems to be blighted in the bud. All this casts a shadow over our spontaneous turning to God our Father. Our prayer may be, momentarily at least, afflicted by despair, disillusionment, and self-doubt. How can we ask God to exercise his providence in cases where we human beings are so culpably ineffective and self-serving?

In these and other less dramatic moments we become painfully aware of the ambiguity and ambivalence of human good will. No man or woman is ever totally good or totally bad. There is always some goodness to be found among evil deeds, while even the best of our good deeds are flawed by some degree of self-interest. 'Your Father knows these things', said Jesus; yet we pray 'Give us this day our daily bread'. Our Father also knows the clay we are made of, yet we are to pray 'Forgive us our trespasses'.

Prayer for forgiveness is, of course, prayer of petition, but it is not generally thought to be theologically problematic. Indeed it would appear to be the easiest to understand and accept of all the petitions of the Lord's Prayer. After all, we are not looking for a 'miracle', when we pray for forgiveness, and we do not even have to add 'if it be your will', since God has revealed his desire and willingness to forgive. There is no danger of triviality, superstition, or magic here – or is there?

We have already considered the meaning of divine justice and how easily our idea of it is distorted by human meanness of spirit. If divine justice is taken to be vengeful and despotic, then prayer for forgiveness will be hectic, craven, and perhaps even despairing. Forgiveness is the foundation of Christian spirituality, for the Christian is by definition a forgiven sinner. We pray for forgiveness because God, while never ceasing to offer it, neither forces it on anyone nor grants it automatically. The prayer ensures that our part in what is taking place will always be a thoroughly human and fully conscious one.

Prayer for forgiveness is a play in two acts. The first act consists in coming before a Father who understands not merely the offences we have committed and the good we have left undone but also the state of mind and emotions of us who have offended and now seek to be reconciled.

Many Christians see the play, or at least their part in it, as ending at this point. They are conscious that God forgives their sins but less conscious, perhaps, that he forgives *them*. For a variety of reasons, of which the most significant has been sacramental practice, Catholics have been taught to focus their attention upon the offences rather than upon the person who commits the offences. Unreformed moral theology classified sins into mortal and venial, with many further sub-divisions. The diagnostic tests were largely external – conformity or lack of conformity with a clearly defined list of injunctions. There was a recognition of certain possibly extenuating circumstances of a subjective nature, *e.g.*, lack of advertence or consent, which could make the difference between mortal and venial sin. This is not the place to enter into discussion of either moral theology or confessional practice.

I am less concerned with the legalism, the element of calculation, and the sheer externalism which often prevailed, than with the diversion of attention away from the therapeutic character of consciously receiving God's loving forgiveness. To be sure, it was professed as a theory; but the system in which it was enshrined militated against its practice. Moralists were so busy cataloguing and grading the sins that they never got round to considering the problem of how the sinner should receive the forgiveness offered. They constantly overlooked the practical implications of the truth they professed in theory, namely, that it takes a living faith to accept God's acceptance. The prevailing model of the sacrament of forgiveness was forensic. The drama was sited in the courtroom where the divine judge, acting through the instrumentality of his earthly representative, declared a sentence of remittance. The debt was declared basically cancelled by the judge. But judges do not normally embrace those they have discharged. They neither run out of their courtrooms in search of criminals to be forgiven nor throw parties to celebrate the acceptance and healing of a broken man or woman. In short, the forensic model of divine forgiveness is so defective that it actually distorts the glorious character of what is going on when sinners turn in faith to the God who not merely created them but adopts them into sonship and daughterhood.

The second act of the drama is where the deepest work is done. God has forgiven me; but have I forgiven myself? God accepts me; but do I accept myself? The remittance of a list of offences does not of itself fit me for the forgiveness and acceptance of my fellow men and women. Only a deep awareness of divine acceptance can do that. For we pray 'Forgive us our trespasses as we forgive those who trespass against us'. This petition should not be taken as asking God to forgive us *in the measure* of our forgiveness of others. Our forgiveness of others, like everything else we do, is flawed and very imperfect. Luke's version of the Lord's Prayer gives the petition thus: 'Forgive us our sins, for we ourselves forgive every one who is indebted to us' (Luke 11:4). The point is clear enough. We may not dissociate God's forgiveness of us from our forgiveness of each other. To stand before God asking for his forgiveness and acceptance implies willingness to share that forgiveness and acceptance with others. 'Because you have loved me you have made me lovable', St Augustine says to God. Now, one cannot be lovable without being loving. It would be sheerest hypocrisy to ask for God's acceptance while consciously refusing acceptance to those who are, expressly or by implication, asking to be accepted by us. It is God's acceptance of us which makes our acceptance of each other both possible and mandatory.

> Just as it is true that the hateful and unforgiving man is incapable
> of reconciliation with God, it is equally true that our disposition
> to forgive is based upon the restoring and forgiving love of God.
> True forgiveness is only possible in a true community.[2]

Like the prayer for our daily bread, the prayer for divine forgiveness has political and social consequences. 'True forgiveness is only possible in a true community.' To ask for forgiveness is to express one's willingness to belong to an accepting community, *i.e.*, to a gathering of those who are celebrating their acceptance by God in Christ by creating a community where every member accepts, or strives to accept, every other member. That is what we mean, or should mean, by 'Church'. It is the gathering of forgiven sinners who are commissioned to cooperate with the Holy Spirit in bringing about the Kingdom of God. Time and again throughout the Christian centuries the Church as institution has in practice identified itself with the Kingdom, thereby sealing itself off from reform and renewal and accepting, as God-willed, conditions such as establishment by the State which were institutionally favourable to it.

Ever since the conversion of Constantine in the early fourth century, the Church as institution has, from time to time, sought, or simply accepted the offer of, favours from the State. These favours allowed the Church to pray in security, but often at the price of keeping silent about political and social injustice. The situation arises today in countries where an oppressive government maintains in power a small number of very rich citizens and buys the silence of the Church by offering it institutional advantages. Since in these circumstances prayer for daily bread and for forgiveness has a hollow ring to it, small groups

2. John Lowe, *The Lord's Prayer*, Oxford, Clarendon Press, 1962, p. 42.

of Christians have been driven by the exigencies of prayer itself to separate themselves from the complicity of the institution by setting up small communities devoted to action on behalf of the oppressed and the dispossessed.

Circumstances differ from country to country, and we should be slow to pronounce on situations in which we ourselves are not actively involved. Every country has its own share of deprived and alienated men and women. In every country the prayer for daily bread is, or should be, a reminder of the needs of the poor and hungry. In every country the prayer for forgiveness should be a call to remember the plight of those who are alienated for one or other of a hundred possible reasons. Social and economic deprivation is not the only cause of alienation in its deepest sense.

It is perhaps when we are most aware of our political and social responsibilities and are doing something to discharge them, that we most experience the frustration of impotence in the face of the world's inequities and injustices. It is all too easy to lose hope at the sight of so much oppression and man-made suffering. This, as Christians, we cannot allow ourselves to do. In spite of everything, 'in all these things we are more than conquerors through him who loved us' (Romans 8:37). Our prayer has to reflect St Paul's quiet and deep confidence in the Christ who has conquered.

There are many battles yet to be fought, but the war has been won in principle. We can with profit practise what George Tyrrell called 'provisional pessimism', *i.e.*, the sort of attitude that refuses to indulge in the superficial optimism which besets certain kinds of liberal humanism. The kind of 'pessimism' recommended by Tyrrell might also be called 'transcendental optimism', in that it is open-eyed and realistic about the human condition. It accepts with Pascal that humanity is the glory and the scandal of the universe. We belong to a race that builds hospitals – and concentration camps. As Pascal also pointed out, we are a mystery to ourselves; and that mystery lies at the heart of our prayer. Our response to it is likely to be wordless and disconsolate. St Augustine saw this state of mind and heart as the raw material of prayer.

For in most cases prayer consists more in groaning than in speaking, in tears rather than in words. But [God] sets our tears in his sight, and our groaning is not hidden from him who made all things by the Word, and does not need human words.[3]

God was not content simply to create all things through his Word. He sent his Word to *be* one of us; and we did to him what we had done to the prophets and continue to do to the weak, the poor, the powerless, and the outcasts of this world. In nailing Jesus of Nazareth to the Cross our race did the worst it could do to the divine order of the universe. On that afternoon on a hill outside Jerusalem our customary inhumanity to our brothers and sisters became our inhumanity to God. And by that act we were reconciled to the Father who instead of annihilating the universe as a monstrous failure of design and execution gave us the Cross as a sign of hope. Through it God says to us, 'This is the worst you can do – and yet I *still* love you, because my Son is one of you.' We did it to God's Son thinking him to be merely one of our own. He *was* one of our own, but not merely one of our own. By undergoing what we, his brothers and sisters, inflicted on him, he fulfilled all the purposes of creation. With the author of the Fourth Gospel we call him the Word of God. But because the Word became flesh he was also the most perfect possible answer to that Word. He laid aside all the glorious prerogatives of the divine Word and assumed all the seemingly inglorious uncertainties of the human answer. The constant teaching of the Eastern Fathers of the Church has been expressed in a statement from which the Western mind has shrunk in pious and false humility: *God became human so that we might become divine.*

It is from the depths of our humanity that we make our petitions. So too did Jesus who,

> in the days of his flesh, offered up prayers and supplications, with loud cries and tears, to him who was able to save him from death, and he was heard in his godly fear. Although he was a Son, he learned obedience through what he suffered; and being made perfect he became the source of eternal salvation to all who obey him; being designated by God a high priest after the order of Melchizedek (Hebrews 5:7-10).

---

3. Letter 130, X, 20.

# Acknowledgements

IN 1979, Mater Dei Institute in Dublin invited me to read a paper to teachers of religion on the prayer of petition. That was later published in *Doctrine & Life*. Then editor and publisher, Austin Flannery, O.P., along with American publisher Michael Glazier suggested that I write a book on the subject.

The opening chapter, 'Knowing God', is based on a paper I gave at the Maynooth Summer School in 1978, later published in *The Furrow*. I am grateful to Ronan Drury, editor of *The Furrow*, for permission to use it in a new form here.